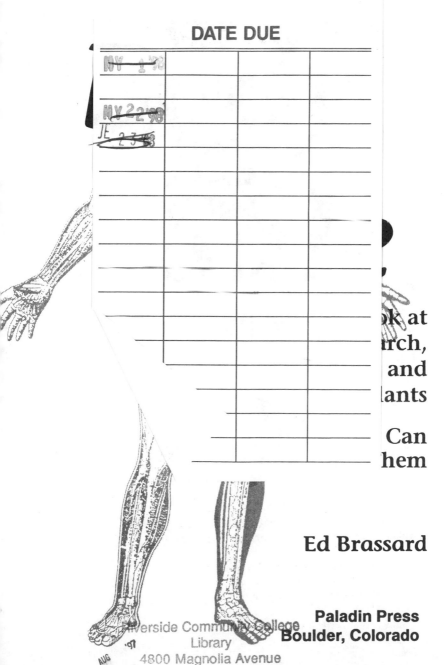

DATE DUE

NY 1 98			
NY 2 2 98			
JE 2 3 98			

ok at
rch,
and
lants

Can
hem

Ed Brassard

Paladin Press
Boulder, Colorado

Body for Sale:
An Inside Look at Medical Research, Drug Testing, and Organ Transplants
& How You Can Profit from Them
by Ed Brassard

ISBN 0-87364-858-7
Printed in the United States of America

Published by Paladin Press, a division of
Paladin Enterprises, Inc., P.O. Box 1307,
Boulder, Colorado 80306, USA.
(303) 443-7250

Direct inquiries and/or orders to the above address.

Contents

Acknowledgments

I would like to thank those people who have helped in making this book possible:

Doug Fouquet and **Debbi Brassard**, for the many long nights we worked together; **Beverly Trainer**, who shared my enthusiasm in exploring this subject and did extensive writing and research for this book; another collaborator, **Susan Duerkson** and **Rex Dalton**, medical writers for the *San Diego Union-Tribune*; and **Judy Erickson,** reporter for the *Escondido Times-Advocate*. Susan and Judy wrote major stories that helped create national attention for my idea. Rex, a pro in medical research reporting, provided much helpful information. I also wish to thank **Dr. Brian Blackborne,** San Diego County coroner; **Dr. Andrea Podolsky** from Vienna, Austria; **Victoria Leeyer,** owner of Surrogate Parenting; and **John Coleman,** my graphic artist. Finally, my special thanks to **Paladin Press** for believing in me and making this book possible.

To my daughter, Kristiana, and my wife, Debbi.

Introduction

"WANTED:
WE ARE LOOKING FOR A FEW GOOD PEOPLE."

Have you ever sat down and wondered how much you were really worth, dead or alive? There are people around this world who are looking for you. What makes this world turn round? People, money, and medical research.

Why pay doctors for an office visit when they can pay *you* for the visit? Every day on TV, in the newspapers, or in the schools, you see ads promising:

> *Earn extra money. Be part of a research study.*
> *Make $250, just call . . .*
> *If you have insomnia, we will pay $1,000.*
> *Have asthma? Will pay $500.*

Some research subjects can make $5,000 to $10,000 doing just one study. There is also a rumor that there is one research study out there that will pay you $25,000 if you're willing to let them stop your heart for two minutes. Playing the research market can lead to a nice income.

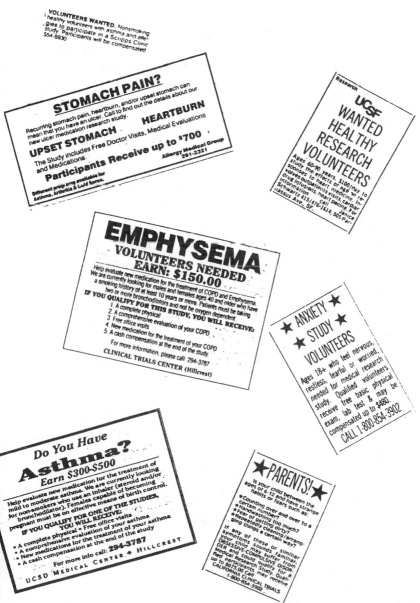

THE ULTIMATE JUNKYARD—YOUR BODY PARTS

Dead or alive, your body can be worth more than $100,000 if it's put to the right use. There is also a market for body parts. Imagine being able to purchase needed organs the same way you'd buy used car parts from the local junkyard. This practice may well become a reality in the not-too-distant future. At the moment people are being paid a fair amount of money to donate their time, effort, and sometimes precious body parts to benefit science—a practice that in the future could allow us to exchange our old, broken-down organs for nice, new healthy ones. Think what this could mean for senior citizens! Certainly, this is an issue rife with controversy.

But, alas, politics gets, and always will get, involved, sometimes preventing lifesaving organs from reaching those in need. In spite of heated debates, many thousands of lives are being saved every day by transplants that even as recently as 10 years ago would have been impossible. As medical technology advances, attitudes will change, and a new set of ethics will evolve. But not without new questions and conflicts—the traditional price of progress.

This book will not attempt to address the moral dilemma surrounding this debatable subject. Rather, it will inform those who are interested in becoming research subjects or organ donors. By sharing with you my experiences as a human guinea pig, together with in-depth interviews with physicians and researchers, I hope to give you a detailed perspective on what to expect. For those who are interested and sincerely motivated, I think you'll find this information enlightening, instructive, and even financially rewarding. But most important, you will know that with every study in which you participate, you are making a contribution to your fellow human beings. And in the grand scheme of things, isn't that what our purpose on Earth is all about?

Chapter 1   HUMAN GUINEA PIGS

Every year more than a million medical research studies take place in the United States and Canada. Newspapers and university bulletin boards run ads offering cash incentives and free medical treatment to qualified volunteers. But the big money goes into the deep pockets of doctors, researchers, foundations, attorneys, and pharmaceutical companies.

Although nonprofit organizations and drug companies contribute generously to the cost of testing new and more promising drugs, government grants account for more than $30 billion annually to research institutions, universities, and labs throughout the country.

The low-end cost for a research trial is about $150,000. For more complex projects, the figure can run into the millions. The pharmaceutical industry has become a $50 billion a year business, with the stakes climbing ever higher.

MY LIFE AS A RESEARCH SUBJECT

My experience with research studies began in 1981 when I went to an emergency room with severe stomach pain. To everyone's surprise I was diagnosed with an ulcer—at age 18! The doctor handed me some medication and suggested I look into an ongoing ulcer study at a local university.

WANTED: WE NEED YOUR BODY!
WANT TO BE IN A RESEARCH STUDY?

DO YOU HAVE ALLERGIES? HOW ABOUT A HARD TIME SLEEPING AT NIGHT? MAYBE A LITTLE DEPRESSION?

Did you know that there are doctors, researchers, and hospitals out there that will pay you for your little problems?

If you are 6 months to 100 years old you may qualify to be in a medical reseach study....and you may make from $5 to $15,000 just to be in one study!

MEN		WOMEN		CHILDREN	
Asthma	$250-500	Asthma	$250-500	Allergy	$100-150(Or Free Care)
Anxiety	$50-480	Allergy	$50-250	Child Development Study	$20
Blood	$20-75	Blood	$20-100	Hypertension Syndrome	$20-200
Depression	$50-1000	Depression	$50-1000	Learning Study Brain Waves	$20 (Free Toys)
Emphysema	$150	Eggs (each)	$2000-3000		
Fungus (Big Toe)	$150	Heart Burn	$100-700		
Insomnia (per night)	$100-300	Insomnia (per night)	$100-300		
Sperm (per shot)	$45	Rh-Sensitized Mothers	$200+		
Upset Stomach	$200-700	Yeast Infection	$100		

MAN   WOMAN   CHILD

HUMANS FOR HIRE

Stories by JUDY ERICKSON and E'LOUISE ONDASH

THIS IS ONLY A TEST...

 d Brassard has learned not to count on the extra income every month, but the Del Mar resident also knows that being a human guinea pig can sometimes pay enough to cover his car payments and then some.

By frequently vol- unteering for medical studies — occasional- ly two or three at a time — the 29-year- old nuclear energy service technician says he makes up to $5,000 a year. Besides the stipends, Bras- sard is lured by free tests, medications, care by the experts — even free movie tick- ets and vacations.

Since volunteering for his first study 10 years ago, Brassard has participated in:

■ A stomach ulcer study that included the insertion of a tube down his throat to photograph the stom- ach lining. "They se- date you with Valium so you don't care. You

Please see TEST, D3 ▶

After some consideration, I decided to sign up. I was offered a cash compensation for allowing a doctor to insert an endoscopic tool (a tubular minicamera) down my throat to inspect the inner walls of my stomach. This rather uncomfortable procedure confirmed the emer- gency room diagnosis: I definitely had a peptic ulcer—a dubious distinction that qualified me to try an experi- mental drug that, it was hoped, would alleviate my symptoms. To my great delight, the medication fulfilled its promise and put an end to my complaints.

A few years later I made a grand tour of Europe—on a shoestring. While visiting Munich, I would hang out at the university where I could grab a meal at student prices. One fellow I became acquainted with happened to men- tion that there were four medical studies in progress at the school, and they were in need of volunteers.

I did some investigating and learned that I qualified for two of them: an allergy study and one involving eye- blinking. Both trials lasted two weeks, and I was paid 200 deutsche marks (approximately US$130). As before, I found the studies both interesting and helpful, a novel sort of part-time work.

When I moved back to California, I ended up living near La Jolla, the home of polio vaccine discoverer Jonas Salk. La Jolla is an elegant coastal community and one of the world's leading centers of medical research. There are four research institutes and four major hospitals within a three-mile radius.

Although I was busy with a full-time job, I managed to participate in some 40 studies that first year. Because I'm extremely health conscious, I was selective about the studies to which I subjected myself. I read extensively about each one before enrolling and learned how to gauge what was an acceptable risk. I participated in everything from a skin cream trial to a sleep study that required three nights in the hospital. During the course of a year I made about $5,000, received free medical care, and enjoyed the idea that I was helping my fellow man by contributing to medical history.

I also found myself afflicted with a full-blown case of curiosity. The more studies I participated in, the more I wanted to know why certain tests were conducted, who benefited, and who really pulled the strings in this cutting-edge, billion-dollar industry.

Some degree of controversy always exists when human beings are used as guinea pigs, even in the best-case scenarios. It would be ideal, of course, if we could confine medical research to test tubes and computer simulations. Animal activists would prefer that scientists use no animal models, and no one really wants to subject men, women, and children to untried medications.

But there is simply no other way. Test tubes and laboratory rats can provide only limited information. Eventually every new drug must undergo human trials. Not to conduct such experiments is unthinkable; without them we would be deprived of drugs that save lives, prevent illness, and relieve pain and suffering.

So who goes first? Who gets the honor of serving as a trial balloon? In the past, prison inmates and, in some cases, retarded or illiterate subjects have been used in medical experiments, with or without their consent and often without a full understanding of the risks involved. Over the years most such travesties have been eliminated by laws that protect individuals to the fullest degree possible. But safety nets weren't constructed overnight, and as with most human endeavors, progress has usually been nudged along by scandal.

When you visit a doctor and become a patient, you can be pretty well assured that your welfare (along with his or her fee) is the prime objective. But subjects in medical trials must realize that the discovery of new information is the foremost goal.

From the fifteenth century to the present, research has enabled mankind to chart the future and improve the quality of life. Almost anything is possible with the human body. Ethical or unethical, medical research is a source of life and death, hope and new beginnings, and, for some, an extremely profitable venture.

A BILLION-DOLLAR BUSINESS

Every year our government hands out around $187 billion in medical research grants. Thousands of institutions, schools, and labs are applying for these grants every day. One good allergy study can bring in $150,000, and a few studies register in the millions. Not all grants come from the government; many are from private pharmaceutical companies and nonprofit organizations. The business of putting new pills on the market is one of the fastest-growing industries in the world and one of the most complex.

In the 1990s, the pharmaceutical industry has become one of the nation's most profitable businesses, bringing in some $55 billion every year. The money comes from both government and private funding. Patients with a variety of medical problems all rely on medications that improve the quality of their lives—and, in some cases, enable their lives to continue. The individuals mentioned below have two things in common: they have benefited from medical research, and they owe their lives or well-being to drugs.

- Jim Cook, an accountant in his 40s, suffers from diabetes, a stomach ailment, and high blood pressure. To control these conditions he takes prescription drugs that cost $150 a month—more than he spends for food or a week's rent.
- Ed Johnson, a transplant patient, takes pills to keep his new heart from being rejected. The cost is around $50 a day.
- When Don Forest suffered a heart attack, emergency-room doctors treated him with a new, highly acclaimed clot-busting drug. The treatment cost $2,200.
- Debbie Small has a potentially lethal ailment called Gaucher's disease, which weakens bones and causes painful swelling of the spleen. Her medication runs a whopping $270,000 a year.
- Tom Malcolm came down with AIDS and is on a daily regimen of AZT in hopes of slowing the progression of the disease. The initial price for AZT treatment was set at around $10,000.

DRUG DEVELOPMENT AND TESTING

Every day pharmacists fill prescriptions for people suffering from a variety of ailments. About 1.6 billion prescriptions are filled each year in the United States alone—seven for every man, woman, and child.

New drugs are constantly being discovered and developed to cure disease and improve our quality of life. The responsibility for this huge task has fallen largely on the shoulders of the pharmaceutical industry.

But where do drugs come from? How are they discovered, developed, and tested? And, more important, what part do you play in the process?

Discovering New Drugs

The process begins when research scientists discover a promising compound and begin testing it in laboratory experiments. This sounds easier than it actually is; as recently as 50 years ago, discovering a new drug was like finding a needle in a haystack. Usually tens of thousands of compounds would be tested, with little notion of what might result, before a promising drug candidate was finally unearthed.

Today, with greater knowledge of how the human body works, researchers can better concentrate on discovering compounds that alter or regulate the body's natural biological processes.

Testing

Once a potential drug is discovered, it goes through a development and testing period that is carefully regulated by the Food and Drug Administration (FDA). First, the drug company does experiments in test tubes to see if the potential drug has the desired biological properties.

This is followed by nonclinical testing on animals. Researchers make every effort to use as few animals as possible and to ensure their humane and proper care. These experiments look for harmful effects and try to confirm the drug's potential effectiveness.

If a drug proves safe in animals, the company begins the task of gaining FDA approval to test it in humans. All human testing is conducted only with the informed consent of the volunteer patients and under the guidance of the FDA and an Institutional Review Board (IRB). The IRB consists of members of the community, with both medical and nonmedical backgrounds and with no professional or monetary

COMPOUND TO MARKET

Only about 1 in 5,000 new chemicals discovered in the laboratory ever makes it to patients. The average drug takes 12 years (although some make it in as few as 3) and $359 million to develop.

Discovery

- A drug or a compound is found in laboratory or natural environment, or designed from scratch. This is the most critical stage.

Research and Development

Laboratory Research

- Test-tube studies and research in animal models that mimic the human diseases.

- Testing on rats, monkeys, rabbits, guinea pigs (will the drug work or not?).

- Preclinical tests—laboratory evaluations to assess safety and effectiveness.

Pharmaceutical Companies Develop New Pill

Pre-Human Test Studies

- Company must file an Investigational New Drug (IND) application.

- Companies work on financing and marketing.

- Companies make deal with hospitals and clinical studies facility.

Investors Funding

New Drugs

People wanted for Research Study

Okay from FDA

Released to Public

Clinical Studies

- Phase 1 studies start. Phase 1 is concerned with the safety of the new drug and involves a small number of healthy volunteers (fewer than 20). One- to seven-day study.

- Phase 2 studies start. Patients who actually have the disease or condition are treated. Two to eight weeks.

- Phase 3 studies start. Drug safety and effectiveness are tested. Results sent to FDA for approval. Three weeks to a year or longer.

- Phases 4 and 5 studies start. Takes place after information from Phases 1 through 3 has been submitted to FDA. These studies provide additional information to help use the drug appropriately.

FDA Approval

- From start to finish it can take 3 to 12 years for a pill to make it to market—if it makes it that far.

- Press release announces that new pill is on the market.

- Doctors prescribe pills. Now available at local stores.

13

interest in the drug sponsor or the physician (clinical investigator) conducting the study. The IRB usually averages about eight people, monitors the welfare of study participants by making sure the protocol is appropriate, and ensures that each participant is properly informed.

INFORMED CONSENT

When you agree to participate in a drug study, you are asked to sign an informed-consent form. This document assures the FDA that you've been informed of your rights and are aware of the risks and benefits of participating in the study and that your participation is voluntary.

This form also provides information about the drug and the study procedure in lay terms. It describes the anticipated effects of the drug, including research supporting its safety and effectiveness. The form explains the nature of the study and specific procedures to be followed. It also includes an assurance of confidentiality and a statement of treatment alternatives.

The informed-consent form and the study protocol (which instructs the clinical investigator on how the study is to be conducted) must be reviewed and approved by an IRB before the study can begin.

The IRB must also approve all protocol changes or additions before any alterations in the study can take place. The clinical investigator is obligated to inform the IRB promptly of all serious and unexpected drug side effects, as well as all unanticipated problems involving risk to study participants.

It is important to realize that every beneficial drug also poses certain risks, or side effects. These may be as minor as a dry mouth or an upset stomach, or as major as death. A drug's benefit may range from alleviating chronic pain to curing cancer.

THE ROLE OF THE FDA

The human or "clinical testing" of a new drug is one of the most critical stages of drug development. It is carefully regulated by the FDA, which is responsible for ensuring the safety of study participants, and controlled by the drug company. The FDA requires that pharmaceutical companies supply specific information about the selected clinical investigators, and this information is then reviewed to ensure that these physicians meet FDA standards.

Preclinical testing involves laboratory evaluation of product chemistry and animal studies to assess the potential safety and efficacy of the product. Before starting human clinical testing, a company must file an Investigational New Drug (IND) application and receive no objection from the FDA. This application is a summary of the preclinical studies, and it also includes an in-depth discussion of the human clinical studies being proposed. Testing may begin 30 days after filing an IND, unless the FDA raises questions that must be answered prior to the start of trials.

Drugs are developed to treat many different conditions. The FDA is organized into divisions that correspond to specific diseases and employs specialists within these groups to review the safety and effectiveness of new drugs within their area of expertise.

The FDA review process is thorough and involves close collaboration between it and the drug company. Final FDA approval normally takes several years.

WHAT TO EXPECT FROM A DRUG STUDY

The first day of the study you'll meet the clinical investigator or staff member who will review your medical history and current condition. He or she will describe the study and explain the informed-consent form.

You'll also be given a physical examination. Tests

might involve taking blood and urine samples. You will then receive your first supply of study medication, thorough instructions on how to take it, and any special procedures that must be followed. You may be given the test drug, a placebo, or a drug that is already on the market.

On follow-up visits, you'll discuss with the clinical investigator or staff member what has happened since your last visit and be required to answer several questions: Have you taken any medications other than the study drug? Have you experienced any side effects? Have you undergone any important changes in your life? Have you missed any of your medication? The investigator will review your medication schedule and give you more of either the study drug or a placebo.

As a volunteer, you'll be expected to comply with the study requirements. Basically, this means taking all supplied medication as prescribed and keeping all your scheduled appointments.

Proper compliance assures that the information collected will be accurate and reliable. More important, however, failure to comply may jeopardize your health. Skipping your medication for a day or more may affect your well-being as well as the results of the study.

GETTING INTO A STUDY

With hundreds of studies out there just begging for volunteers, there is plenty of opportunity to make money and reap benefits. Here's what doctors and researchers won't tell you—ways to get yourself selected ahead of others for almost any kind of study you choose. As you read on, this section will explain how you can easily become a "human guinea pig for hire."

Literally, throughout the United States and Canada there are thousands of research studies going on each day, and all of them need volunteers. It has been estimated that at just one hospital more than 30 studies are taking place at any given time, and at several major universities in California that number swells to more than 2,000.

There are so many studies out there, it's hard to keep up with them all. Take a look on page 31 at just a few of them, from A to Z. You can participate in these trials to the extent that you are willing to subject yourself. You can volunteer for free or for fun, for money, or maybe even to help save your own life. You need them, and they need you.

Research has become a part of our everyday life. Just consider the objects in front of your eyes, the furniture you're sitting on, or what you're eating. Each of these items required research to prepare for you, the consumer. And then the product undergoes the ultimate test: if we like it, we buy it. The same principle is true for new drugs. Before a medication can become available for public consumption, it must be tested, first on animals and then on people. This means research studies—and guinea pigs.

WIGGLING YOUR WAY IN

Truth isn't always the surest way to become part of a clinical trial. Many researchers don't like to hear this, but it's part of a game that can be played on both sides. Researchers are always on the lookout for new participants to help with their studies, and it's possible to "wiggle" your way into a study. The screening process can take five minutes or as long as two days. You may not have the precise qualifications they're looking for, but with some know-how and experience, you can often qualify just the same.

People from all walks of life will respond to an ad—men and women, young and old, rich and poor—but not all studies are easy to get into. Let's say you really want to participate in a trial that's going to attract a lot of attention because it is unique or pays especially well; you may need an edge. Take a look at the ad below:

WANTED
Volunteers needed for research study
for Anxiety and Depression.
Participants ages 18 to 65.
Are you feeling depressed, sad, or hopeless?
Loss of interest or energy?
Sleeping too much or too little?
Crying frequently?
Qualified volunteers receive free physical exam, test.
May be compensated up to $1,000.

Almost half the people in the United States and Canada at sometime may feel a little down or depressed, or experience a loss of energy. Well, you may easily be the "half" the researchers are looking for. You call the number listed in the ad and tell the interviewer that you have most of the qualifications mentioned in the ad.

Now the screening process begins. You'll be asked your name and age, where you saw the ad, and if you have 15 minutes to answer questions. The answer to that is always yes. You'll be asked if you are taking any medicines now or have in the past. This is where doing a bit of homework can help you find out what kind of drugs people generally take for depression or mood swings. Some of the drugs now on the market are Prozac, Valium, Lithium, and Elevil.

We all know that medical researchers are testing new drugs that will be similar to pills currently on the market. I'm not suggesting that you say you've been on Prozac or Valium if you've never taken these medications, but it certainly won't hurt to read up on them.

For whatever reason, some people want so badly to be part of a particular project that they will do whatever is necessary to qualify. The following is an actual case history of a young man who "wiggled" his way into a study.

A young man named Alan came across the following ad in his local newspaper:

Volunteers for Research Study, Earn Up to $250
If you suffer from Allergies and are between the ages of 30-45,
call 1-800-123-4567

Before volunteering, Alan decided to call and ask what type of allergies was being studied. Then he read a book on the subject and was well prepared when he placed his second call. After an initial interview, he was granted an appointment for the following day.

At the research center, Alan carefully filled out the paperwork and then was asked to submit a urine sample, have his blood drawn, and undergo an allergy skin test. He knew that the researchers were specifically looking for individuals allergic to grass pollen. Because he had few problems with this type of allergy, when it came time for the skin test Alan feared he might be disqualified if he didn't "help things along."

The doctor pricked his arm 15 times with a pollen serum that would produce either a positive or negative reaction. When the physician left the room, Alan noted that only a few of the spots showed any sign of redness or swelling. He correctly figured that this was not enough of a response for a positive reaction, so he began to rub the sites vigorously. When the doctor came back a few minutes later to check Alan's reaction, he saw several raised red lesions around the test sites on Alan's arm. Alan was thus qualified for the allergy study.

BEFORE YOU TAKE THE PLUNGE

A great many people wish to participate in research studies because they are looking for a new drug that may help cure a particular ailment. Others may have a bit of free time and want to do something constructive. But in most cases people hope to make extra money while doing something interesting and worthwhile.

Before taking the plunge for the first time, you might want to ask yourself the following questions:

- How much time and energy am I willing to invest in a research study? Some require a lengthy time commitment, and others require you to undergo tests and procedures that are uncomfortable or even painful.
- What type of medications am I willing to subject myself to—if any?
- How much money do I feel I would have to make to adequately compensate me for my time, effort, and possible discomfort?

You need to weigh all the risks and benefits carefully before committing. I really want to emphasize this because you may be subjecting yourself to an experience that may or may not be in your best interests, and ultimately YOU are the one who must live with your one and only body for the rest of your life. So gather as much information as you can and then weigh all the considerations carefully before making a decision.

BENEFITS AND BONUSES

The benefits of participating in a study can be multifaceted. The following is an example.

A major newspaper recently ran an ad recruiting insomnia sufferers. The ad led with the question: "Do you have sleep problems?" A 30-year-old man we will call Jim had tried for years to convince his family physician that he had a difficult time falling asleep almost every night. His doctor rationalized that maybe Jim's problem was due to stress or just not being able to "turn his mind off." Jim insisted that he had followed all his doctor's suggestions, including eliminating caffeine, alcohol, and stressful situations before bedtime. But none of these strategies worked, and he pleaded once again for some kind of sleeping pill. But his physician, perhaps overly concerned about addiction, stubbornly refused to write a prescription.

Disappointed by his doctor's lack of responsiveness, Jim decided to enroll in a sleep study at a local university. During the screening process he expressed frustration over his chronic inability to fall asleep. He discovered that the purpose of this trial was to research a new drug not yet on the market that was similar to low-dose Valium or Halcyon. He was excited by the prospect of at long last finding a remedy for his insomnia.

The requirement for the double-blind study was simply to take the medication, as needed, for sleep. One group was given a placebo, and the other received the new drug, with neither the participants nor the researchers aware of who was getting what.

After the four-month study was completed, Jim was paid a total of $350 for his time and effort. But for him the real payoff was an agreement he'd made with the research physicians. To relieve his insomnia, they consented to continue prescribing the medication of his choice.

NO FEMALE RATS

Up until now, women have been largely passed over as subjects in research studies. Part of the reason goes back to the synthetic hormone DES, once used to prevent premature births and miscarriages. In 1971, the medical community and the women who had taken the drug were hit with a bombshell: studies showed that the female offspring of mothers taking the hormone suffered from a high percentage of reproductive disorders and an alarming rate of vaginal cancer.

Fearing another catastrophe, the pharmaceutical industry began excluding all women from research studies except those who were diagnosed as terminal.

The altruistic reason was to avoid causing harm to fetuses; the more pressing motive was to avoid lawsuits.

The result is that today most of the drugs taken by women have been tested only on men. And this phenomenon, of course, produces a variety of risks. In recent years, however, with the growing concern about breast cancer, osteoporosis, and the realization that heart disease in female patients is often misdiagnosed, women's activists have pressured for change.

In 1990 the Congressional Caucus for Women's Issues went into action. The result was a report verifying the fact that the bulk of medical research had been gender discriminatory. Rep. Patricia Schroeder, D–Colo., commented on a series of studies: "The NIH didn't even use female rats!"

But progress is under way. In 1991 came the Women's Health Initiative, and with it the largest study ever undertaken, with a mandatory increase in women participants. And in 1993 the FDA tardily warned drug companies that if "the full range of patients who receive therapy" was not included in trials, applications could be rejected. What this means is that women will have more and more opportunities to participate in research.

Though some experts argue that gender differences are few, the fact is that women consume more drugs than men. And these medications are taken at various times during their menstrual cycles and often in conjunction with prescribed hormones. It's therefore essential that these contingencies be addressed for the ultimate safety and benefit of all women.

Chapter 2   STUDIES PEOPLE DO

MOUNTAIN HIGH

I recently interviewed Andrea Podolsky, MD, an internal medical specialist from Vienna. She was in the United States conducting a study on high-altitude pulmonary edema (HAPE), a disease commonly known as "wet lung." She and her colleagues from the University of California at San Diego and San Francisco selected 13 subjects to participate in a study of the incidence of impaired lung function at high altitudes.

According to Dr. Podolsky, about 2 percent of those who have visited altitudes above 10,000 feet in Europe and North America have developed HAPE. The syndrome impairs breathing and produces a foamy cough. Without treatment, the fluid-filled lungs will cause death.

The requirements for the study were simple: participants were required to be in good health, and at some time in their lives they must have traveled to an altitude of at least 10,000 feet. Six of the subjects had incurred documented cases of HAPE; the remainder had not. The purpose of the trial was to determine if prior HAPE patients would register higher pulmonary artery pressures, which could cause more movement of fluid into the lungs, during exercise than those in the control group.

All those chosen for the study were nicely rewarded. They were paid $500 plus an airline ticket to the White Mountain area of California—almost the equivalent of a paid vacation. But instead of frolicking in the sun, each participant had to undergo the following tests: a plastic catheter was placed in the wrist artery, a second was placed in a vein in the elbow, and a third was used to infuse saline solution and a small amount of soluble gases to measure gas exchange in the lungs.

One of the subjects, Lisa B., was a bit nervous about the procedure, for this was her first study. "At the last minute I got cold feet," she said, "but it was okay because all the catheters were inserted after they gave me a local anesthesia. I'm pretty sensitive to pain, but this was nothing I couldn't handle."

A separate series of tests was performed on Lisa and the others both at sea level and at high altitude. Most of those involved agreed that it was an interesting and worthwhile experience, with a bit of adventure thrown in as a bonus.

POCKET MONEY

Keith S., Age 43

Keith S. lives on the street among the growing ranks of the homeless. Discharged from the army, he now suffers from Post-Traumatic Stress Syndrome (PTSD). He has two incomes: $550 a month disability from the government and whatever he can earn from hiring himself out as a human guinea pig. On the average he participates in five to ten medical studies each month.

Because he is unemployed, Keith is able to pursue this on a full-time basis. Each week he scans the newspaper and often finds 10 to 20 studies going on at once. He calls those that interest him to see if he qualifies. Location isn't a problem because he knows how to get around on the city bus and sometimes he's even reimbursed for his fare. "I enjoy doing the studies," he says, "because I feel I'm contributing to mankind and at the same time I'm helping myself monetarily. It gets me off the streets, doing something worthwhile."

Keith usually tries to seek out a variety of projects. Those he has participated in include a depression study that paid $150 and some cholesterol trials that fetched as much as $250. Not bad for a bus ride.

But it hasn't all been a picnic. "There was one study I did that I'll never forget and I'll never do again," he warns. "It was a cancer study, and they put me up on a table and drilled bone marrow out of my hip. All they gave me was a few shots of local anesthetic and no pain pills to go. And $75 in my pocket. Let me tell you, it wasn't worth it!"

When Keith began interviewing for research studies he found that many screeners disqualified him because he was homeless. He circumvented the problem by offering the address of Friends of Friends in San Diego, an organization that provides a place where the homeless can receive mail or a phone call and spend the day.

A GOOD SLEEP

Don B., Age 36

Don is a photocopier service technician and a chronic insomniac. His relentless tossing and turning caused his wife to banish him to the TV room at night. He has a history of dragging into work with a cup of industrial-strength coffee in hand. Over the years he's sought out a variety of doctors, but none had been able to treat him successfully.

One morning, while groggily pouring through the morning paper, he noticed the following ad:

DO YOU HAVE INSOMNIA?
Problems going to sleep or staying asleep?
If you are a male, 25–65, call to participate
in UCSD research study.
Free physical examination and compensation.

In Don's words, "If they're willing to pay me while they try to solve a problem other doctors can't cure, then it sounds good to me. I contacted them and got myself into the study. I had to sleep in the research lab at the hospital for three nights with a camera looking down at me all night. But I slept! And I made $150 and got a lab report that I can show my family physician. So far I haven't found any magic bullet, but I'm willing to keep trying."

The words of Don B. summarize the attitudes of the majority of research subjects. Though instances of abuse still exist, thanks to watch-dog commissions, they are becoming increasingly rare. For those who are well informed and not in search of a miracle, medical studies can provide significant financial and health benefits as well as an instructive experience.

THE WHITE RAT

Ruth G.

Most study participants are rewarded for their efforts and happy with the results. But what happens when something goes wrong in a trial? Although such instances are rare, once in a while—in spite of all precautions—the dream becomes a nightmare.

Ruth G. of Westport, Connecticut, was more than willing to suffer any inconvenience to get help for the breast cancer that was spreading throughout her body. Conventional therapy had failed, and her only hope was to take an experimental drug or undergo an experimental procedure. But she and her husband, Paul, had no idea how very slim that hope would be.

Even though the couple considered themselves well informed, they failed to anticipate the indifferent nature of medical research. Mrs. G. had hoped to receive caring and comprehensive treatment as part of the clinical study. Instead, in Mr. G.'s words, his wife was "treated like a white rat."

The couple spent thousands of dollars traveling to Texas to participate in an experimental drug trial that sounded promising. After cooperating fully with the daily regime, it became apparent that Mrs. G. was not responding to the medication. Without amenities or the offer of other treatment, she was summarily dismissed. The researchers' attitude, according to Mr. G., seemed to be, "pack up your things and get out today."

Medical experts and ethicists agree that terminal patients like Mrs. G. have become the subjects of choice for today's research. Though their participation in studies may help future patients, the subjects themselves rarely benefit. Ethicists maintain that the desperation of dying patients makes them easily exploitable. The terminally ill do, in fact, make up the first group of humans on whom new drugs are tested.

Although some may rationalize that terminal individuals have nothing to lose, George Annas of the Boston University Schools of Medicine and Public Health disagrees. He recently told the *New York Times* that such patients are indeed at risk because a toxic drug can hasten their death and increase their suffering. Annas would rather see researchers spend more time studying new drugs in the laboratory and on animals than proceed so quickly to human studies. He states, "If no one else would sign up for a study, why use the terminally ill?"[1]

ON THE INFORMATION SUPERHIGHWAY

Another important issue relating to research studies has appeared with the emergence of the information superhighway. In February 1995, the *Wall Street Journal* reported that medical patients who use such on-line computer services as Prodigy can spread untested treatments, questionable practices, and false optimism—and "can even throw drug trials askew by sharing their reactions to medication being tested."

Jack Norton of Minneapolis went on Prodigy after being diagnosed with ALS (Lou Gehrig's disease), organizing other patients to report on new drug trials and the effects they were seeing. "Before this, people just stumbled on trials," said Norton, who urged patients to lobby the National Institutes of Health (NIH) and drug companies to make experimental treatments more widely available.

In 1994 another Prodigy user went on-line with news that a Boston doctor had told a group of patients about Neurontin, an epilepsy drug whose manufacturer believed could aid in ALS cases. Soon, reports of near-miraculous results started appearing on computer screens, as many ALS patients found doctors willing to prescribe Neurontin for them.

Late in 1994, Dr. Robert Miller at California Pacific Medical Center in San Francisco made plans to conduct a formal trial of Neurontin in 150 patients but said he was concerned with the spread of misinformation about the drug. Half the study participants would get placebos, but with Neurontin widely available outside the trial, Miller worries that he may not get enough volunteers who would risk getting the placebo.[2]

WORST-CASE SCENARIO

Usually when a new drug falls short of expectations, it simply fades away with a whimper, not a bang. But occasionally a promising medication appears on the horizon, and rumors of a new "miracle drug" generate great hope and excitement.

This is a story about a man who desperately tried to find a cure for hepatitis B, but unfortunately, according to *Discover* magazine, the drug turned on him. The magazine called it "the worst clinical disaster in recent memory."[3]

Dr. Jay Hoofnagle, leader of the NIH study, called it a "medical nightmare." The drug that had looked so promising was fialuridine, or FIAU, a variant of several of today's prominent AIDS drugs. When FIAU was first tested, it showed little ability to block herpes virus reproduction. Then in the 1980s, Oclassen Pharmaceuticals revived FIAU as a topical treatment for herpes virus infection. Researchers also believed that FIAU could be used to treat serious internal infections.

The company provided FIAU to the NIH in 1990 for a 14-day study of six people infected with both HIV and hepatitis B. According to Dr. Hoofnagle: "We saw the most dramatic inhibition of HIV-hepatitis levels that we have seen with any drug. Within a few days we would see 90 to 95 percent inhibition. Several persons became negative for hepatitis B virus DNA by the end of treatment."

Two more trials were conducted, and the results were again encouraging. So in August 1992, Eli Lilly & Co. bought the overseas rights and agreed to pay for the drug's development and the needed safety tests. The time for long-term human trials was at hand.

Ten patients were enrolled from earlier trials, and five other patients were added for this trial. But soon trouble developed.

The early signs were fatigue, nausea, and vomiting. One man had felt nauseated and tired in the earlier trial, but 75 percent of the virus had cleared from his system, so he volunteered again. But after just a few weeks he experienced wracking abdominal cramps and horrible nausea.

Others also suffered. One experienced severe nausea, and eventually became extremely jaundiced. Another was rushed to a hospital emergency room because his liver had failed, sending his body into shock and causing his other organs to fail. The patient was transferred to the hospital at NIH. There doctors found that despite normal blood tests 10 days earlier, the man was dying. He received an emergency liver transplant but died two days later.

The next day Hoofnagle pulled the files of all 15 patients and took them off the drug. The trial was officially over. Lactic acidosis had caused most of the problems. It resisted the usual treatment, and even after repeated treatments, the patients remained acidotic.

Even after being taken off FIAU, the patients continued to worsen. Another received a liver transplant but died the next day. One with pneumonia died before he could undergo transplantation, and one received a liver transplant and survived only to suffer from severe toxicity symptoms. Two transplants weren't enough to save one female patient. Only one who received a liver transplant did well.

In the case of FIAU, those risks almost paid off. "By four weeks," Hoofnagle said of the final study, "there was a 90-percent inhibition of hepatitis B virus DNA. During the nine weeks of therapy, six of the ten patients became negative."

If researchers could find or develop a drug with FIAU's potency without its toxicity, its potential would be incredible. All these strengths, however, were negated by the drug's fatal weakness.

In a report released by the FDA on FIAU's failure, some of the blame was placed on the FDA's own rules, which do not require doctors to pool data from all their trials until late in the testing. Had the doctors done so, said *U.S. News and World Report*, they might have seen a pattern of similar symptoms and halted the trial sooner.

NOTES

1. Gina Kolata, "When the dying enroll in studies: A debate over false hopes," *New York Times* (29 January 1994): 7.
2. William M. Bulkeley, "E-Mail medicine: Untested treatments, cures find stronghold on on-line services," *Wall Street Journal* (27 February 1995): 1.
3. Larry Thompson, "The Cure That Killed," *Discover* magazine (March 1994): 5.

Chapter 3 A WORLD OF STUDIES

Keep in mind that the several troublesome incidents cited in the previous chapter are rare exceptions to the rule. Most research studies are safe and rewarding. Below is a reference you can use to locate current and ongoing studies on a particular disease.

STUDIES FROM A TO Z

AGING—For information on research studies and publications on health topics of interest to older adults, call 1-800-222-2225.

AIDS—AIDS Clinical Trials Information Service (ACTIS). 1-800-874-2572 or 1-800-TRIALS-A. They have more than 150 research studies on computer and will help you locate a study in your city.

AIDS–CDC NATIONAL AIDS CLEARINGHOUSE—For information on trials for HIV/AIDS or referrals and AIDS programs, call 1-800-458-5231.

ALLERGIES/ASTHMA—Six medical clinics to serve people in California only. Evening appointments available. Call 1-800-300-ASMA.

ALZHEIMER'S—Hot line information on research studies on Alzheimer's and other related disorders, 1-800-438-4380.

ARTHRITIS—For information on arthritis and help in finding a medical research study, call 703-558-8250. Or the National Institute of Arthritis and Musculiskeletal and Skin Diseases will send you information and refer you to a research study. Call 301-495-4484.

ASTHMA—VRG International (formerly National Clinical Research Centers, Inc.) conducts asthma research studies and will even pay you $50 if you refer a friend. Call 1-800-666-7777.

BLOOD—The National Institutes of Health needs blood for its research programs. If you live in Maryland or Washington, D.C., you can receive $45 for one arm, $55 for two arms, and $100 for three hours of your time. Call 1-800-422-6237, 301-496-0092, or 301-496-1048.

CANCER—The National Cancer Institute has information on where new medical research studies can be found. It'll also help you with any other information you may need. Call 1-800-4 CANCER. Boston University Medical Center Clinical Trial Cancer Helplink, 1-800-524-8541 or 1-800-762-6500.

DEPRESSION—A 24-hour information service provides free material on symptoms of depression and where to get treatment. It will also help you find a research study in your city or state. Call 1-800-421-4211.

DIABETES—Operations Coordinating Center is doing research studies coast to coast on Type 1 Diabetes. Just state what city you're in and a representative will tell you which participating doctors are doing studies.

Call 1-800-HALT-DM1 or 1-800-749-7424, ext. 2-7836. Or the National Diabetes Information will help you find research studies on diabetes. Call 310-468-2162.

DRUGS—Food and Drug Administration, Office of Consumer Affairs. The FDA will help you find information on new and old drugs or any other information you may need. 301-443-3170.

EGG DONORS—Mothers only. Carry a child for an infertile couple. Egg donors welcome. Call 1-800-SUR-ROGATE.

EPILEPSY—NIH supports studies at 13 clinical research centers. For information on these centers and possible clinical trials, call 1-800-352-9424 or 1-800-EFA-100.

EYES—NIH conducts research studies involving eyes. Because there are numerous eye disorders, be sure and tell them exactly what you are looking for. Call 301-496-5248.

FERTILITY—For a fertility study in your region, call 212-744-5500 or ACS at 1-800-673-8444.

HEADACHE—For literature on headaches and the best available treatments as well as information on research studies, call 1-800-843-2256.

HEART DISEASE (women)—A research program for women only, known as HERS (Heart and Estrogen-Progestin Replacement Study). There are 15 medical centers across America doing studies on heart disease and post-menopausal women. If you have had a heart attack or bypass surgery and are under 76 years old, call 619-534-8060.

HERPES—For more information on herpes, the American Social Health Association (ASHA) will send you a resource book and will help you find a research study for herpes and other sexually transmitted diseases. Call 1-800-230-6039. For treatment studies, call 919-361-8488.

KIDNEY—NIH will provide information on kidney diseases, transplant information, and research studies. Call 301-496-3583.

LIVER DISORDERS—NIH will send you information and refer you to organizations that will assist you in locating a research study. Call 301-496-3583.

LUNGS—Barnes West County Hospital in St. Louis has 16 hospitals that work with it on medical research studies. At this time they have nine studies in progress, lasting from six months to two years. Their studies range from allergies to lung disorders. They are also looking for kids ages 12 to 17. Call 1-800-243-LUNG or 1-800-967-7400.

MARROW—National Marrow Donor Program is looking for volunteers to donate marrow and will help you find a convenient center. They may also help you find a research study. Call 1-800-366-6711 or 1-800-MAR-ROW-2.

MULTIPLE SCLEROSIS—NIH is seeking ways to prevent and treat multiple sclerosis and supports projects at seven clinical research centers in the United States. For information, call NIH at 1-800-352-9424 or the Multiple Sclerosis organizations in New York (1-800-344-4867), New Jersey (1-800-833-4MSA), or Florida (1-800-441-7055).

PMS—Madison Pharmacy Associates has hopeful and helpful information on premenstrual syndrome. Bimonthly newsletter and information on research. Call 1-800-558-7046.

PROSTATE—VRG International has clinical research centers in 14 cities doing studies year round. Just call and ask for a study in the city nearest to you; also inquire about the $50 referral bonus. Call 1-800-666-7777.

SCHIZOPHRENIA—Do you or someone you love suffer from schizophrenia? Volunteers ages 12 and up may qualify for a medical research study. California Clinical Trials has a number of studies in progress. In California only, call 1-800-854-3902.

SLEEP—The National Sleep Foundation can give you information on sleeping disorders. It has a listing of accredited centers coast to coast. Many of the centers are in hospitals that conduct research studies for sleep. Call 202-785-2300. In Missouri, contact the University of Missouri Sleep Disorders Center at 1-800-ADD-SLEEP.

STROKE—The National Institute of Neurological Disorders and Stroke (NINDS) will help you find a research study on stroke and neurological disorders. It has information on prevention, diagnosis, and treatment. Ask about off-campus studies. Many strokes can be prevented by learning about warning signs and risk factors. NINDS asks that you fax your questions to 301-402-2186 or call 1-800-352-9424.

NATIONWIDE INFORMATION

GENERAL HEALTH—The National Health Hot Line provides information on research studies throughout the United States. State what kind of studies you are looking for or inquire about any health problem. Call 1-800-336-4797.

NIH INFORMATION HOT LINE—Will help you find information on any diseases currently under investigation by NIH or NIH-supported scientists and important health-related topics. You can inquire about anything from abetalipoproteinemia to zoonoses studies. Call 301-496-1766.

PHARMACEUTICAL RESEARCH AND MANUFAC-TURERS OF AMERICA—Free booklet on research in America. Information about new drugs being developed. 1100 15th Street, N.W., Washington, D.C. 20077-2093, or call 1-800-538-2692.

PHARMACO DYNAMICS RESEARCH, INC.—Has an on-line unlimited research studies list. You can call 24 hours a day and find almost any study that exists. In Texas call 1-800-866-0492 or 512-462-0492, ext. 7928.

FREE DRUGS

Most people may not realize that pharmaceutical manufacturers and labs will often provide drugs free of charge to the indigent or those at the poverty level. "This is good news for many people on limited incomes," said Lisa Carr of the Pharmaceutical Manufacturers Association, whose member companies offer some 65 different free drug programs for low-income individuals.

Since many people can't afford some of the more expensive prescription drugs (some cost several dollars per pill), it is good to find that drug manufacturers are willing to help. Later in the chapter a list of contacts to help you locate sources of free drugs is provided. The letter below is typical of what you might receive, along with an application form:

Pharmacia
Patient Assistance Program
P.O. Box 9525
McLean, VA 22102

Dear Mr. Pilleater:

Pharmacia, Inc. provides temporary assistance for medications free of charge to qualified patients. Although the company is committed to providing assistance to as many patients as possible, limited resources are available, and applications will be considered on the basis of greatest need.

To get a patient enrolled in the Patient Assistance Program, the physician's office must call 1-800-366-5570 to see if the patient qualifies for the assistance program. After this initial process, an application is then mailed to the physician's office (all correspondence and drug shipments must be sent to the physician's office). For the application to be considered, your physician must first complete the physician information on the front side of the application. The remainder of the application must be completed by the patient and returned in the postage-paid envelope that is enclosed with each application.

If you have any questions concerning the Patient Assistance Program, please call one of our Information Specialists at 1-800-366-5570.

Sincerely,

Pharmacia, Inc.

The following are a just a few of the drugs currently being offered:

ADRIAMYCIN/PFS (doxorubicin)—Acute lymphoblastic leukemia, Hodgkin's disease, thyroid cancer

ADRUCIL/(Fluonuracil, 5-FU)—Colon cancer, breast cancer

AZULFIDINE/EMCYT/FOLEX PFS/METHOTREXATE, MTX—Ulcerative colitis, prostate cancer, lung cancer, lymphoma (combination therapies)

NOT APPROVED YET!

The following drug companies and manufacturers are testing drugs that have not been approved by the FDA for sale in the United States. However, the manufacturers are making them available at no charge for people who need them. Because the drugs are still in the testing phase, you may be required to record and report side effects and lab results while using them. You may also be asked to have your doctor call the drug company. For specific criteria, call the number listed below.

Pfizer	1-800-742-3029
Bristol-Myers Squibb	1-800-842-8036
Burroughs Wellcome Co.	1-800-722-9294—92
Astra	1-800-388-4148
Glaxo Research	1-800-248-9757
Parke-Davis	1-800-755-0120
Smith-Kline Beecham	1-800-366-8900
Pharmacia	1-800-795-9759 or
	1-800-366-5570
Schering-Plough .	1-800-521-7157
US Bioscience	1-800-537-9978
LaRoche Research Labs	1-800-285-4484

RESEARCH STUDIES IN CANADA

In Canada, there is a variety of research studies being conducted every day. The Medical Research Council (MRC) of Canada, located in Ottawa, is similar to the National Institutes of Health in the United States. The MRC makes development and program grants, collaborates with Canadian universities and industries, and maintains exchange programs with countries in Europe, Asia, and South America.

Besides the MRC, research programs—often involving human subjects—are also funded by provinces, universities, foundations, and private companies. Here is a partial list of granting agencies in Canada:

Addiction Research Foundation of Ontario
33 Russell St.
Toronto, ON M5S 2S1

Alberta Cancer Board
6th Fl., Capital Place
9707 – 110 St.
Edmonton, AL T5K 2L0

Alberta Foundation for Medical Research
3125 ManuLife Place
10180 – 101 St.
Edmonton, AL T5J 3S4

Alzheimer Society of Canada
Ste. 201, 1320 Yonge St.
Toronto, ON M4T 1X2

Arthritis Society
Ste. 901, 250 Bloor St., East
Toronto, ON M4W 3P2

B.C. Health Research Foundation
Ste. 919, 4710 Kingsway
Burnaby, BC V5H 4M2

Canadian Cystic Fibrosis Foundation
Ste. 601, 2221 Yonge St.
Toronto, ON M4S 2B4

Fonds de la recherche en sante du Quebec
Bureau 1950
550, rue Sherbrooke ouest
Montréal (Québec) G1X 4G6

Health Canada/Santé Canada
National Health Research & Development
Holland Cross
Tower A, 2nd Fl.
11 Holland Ave.
Ottawa, ON K1A 1B4

Heart and Stroke Foundation of Canada
Ste. 200, 160 George St.
Ottawa, ON K1N 9M2

Manitoba Health Research Council
Room P127, 770 Bannatyne Ave.
Winnipeg, MB R3E 0W3

National Cancer Institute of Canada
Ste. 200, 160 George St.
Toronto, ON M4V 3B1

**Vancouver Foundation: B.C. Medical Services
Foundation and W.J. VanDusen Foundation**
Ste., 230, One Bentall Centre
505 Burrard St.
Vancouver, BC V7X 1M3

ETHICS OF HUMAN TESTING

The ethical issues involving medical research are ongoing and will probably never be resolved to everyone's satisfaction. But we've at least come a long way from the grim days of human experimentation during Nazi Germany and the reports of secret radiation tests that recently made headlines in the United States.

In 1969 and 1970, the American Academy of Arts and Sciences sponsored a landmark investigation of the ethics of human experimentation. From that study, many of our present guidelines were defined. Edited by Harvard Law School professor Paul Freund, the study stated:

> Today, when the news media feature reports of efforts to prolong life through new surgical techniques involving human organ transplants, public attention is increasingly focused on . . . vital problems . . . One need only refer to the years of Nazi "science" to recall a darker side of the subject.

By the late 1950s, public funds for medical research had escalated to the point where the use of human subjects had reached an unprecedented scale. The first human liver transplant took place in 1963, followed by the first lung transplant in 1964. And 1978 was a banner year: a test-tube baby was born in England.

Each of these accomplishments reflected years of extensive research. As the demand for more experimentation developed, so too did the demand for a better way to evaluate the ethics involved.

In a disturbing 1966 report, Dr. Henry Beecher of Massachusetts General Hospital examined 22 cases of unethical or questionable studies and concluded, "It is evident that in many, the investigators have risked the health or life of their subjects. . . . Evidence is at hand that many of the patients never had the risk satisfactorily explained to them . . . further hundreds have not known that they were the subjects of an experiment."

Beecher also noted that the use of prisoners, which dates back to 1721 when King George I pardoned prisoners who submitted to smallpox inoculations, presents special problems: "The very invitation to participate may function as a bribe, if the rewards are excessive. This destroys the whole concept of free consent."

THE ARRIVAL OF PENICILLIN

The first U.S. clinical tests of penicillin were reported in 1941, and by 1943 there was tremendous need for the drug as soldiers returned from the Pacific with unhealed fractures, osteomyelitis, and long-established infections. The results of penicillin treatment were so encouraging that within weeks, more studies were planned in 10 U.S. Army hospitals.

The trouble was, penicillin was in short supply. In North Africa medics had to make the hard choice between curing gonorrhea or treating war injuries. While many opted for treatment of battle wounds, the Theatre Surgeon elected to make the new wonder drug available to casualties of the brothels. The results were dramatic. Within a week, VD patients no longer overcrowded the military hospitals, and they were able to return to the battlefront in good health.

400 INFECTED BLACK MEN

But on a darker note, we must not forget the notorious U.S. Public Health Service syphilis study that began in 1932. Four hundred poor, illiterate, and infected black men were promised free treatment for their disease. What they received were spinal taps with no anesthesia. And, most horrific, in the 1940s when penicillin would have quickly ended their suffering, researchers chose to *withhold* treatment so they could monitor the progression of the disease.

From the standpoint of concerned citizens who protested this syphilis study once the facts emerged, the Public Health Service was playing fast and loose with the lives of these men to indulge scientific curiosity: "Not since the Nuremberg trials of Nazi scientists had the American people been confronted with a medical cause célèbre that captured so many headlines and sparked so much discussion. For many it was a shocking revelation of the potential for scientific abuse in their own country."[1]

In 1974, two years after this atrocity surfaced, the National Commission for the Protection of Human Subjects of Biomedical and Behavioral Research was formed. Its aims were to ensure that all studies would benefit the subjects involved—as well as society—and to create Institutional Review Boards across the country to oversee medical trials. Although this was a major step, all systems are still subject to the vagaries of the individuals involved.

TOP SECRET:
GOVERNMENT TESTING ON U.S. CITIZENS

In 1951, near Newport News, Virginia, the U.S. Army released an organism called *Aspergillus fumigatus* at the Norfolk Naval Supply Center. Most of the workers there were African-Americans. "Since Negroes are more susceptible to coccioides than are whites," a report stated, "this fungus disease was simulated by using *Aspergillus fumigatus.*" This organism has also been known to cause lethal infections.

Also starting around this time and for 20 years afterward, the army again released bacteria, this time among millions of unsuspecting civilians. At hearings in 1977, Pentagon witnesses acknowledged that bacteria and chemical particles were sprayed over San Francisco, St. Louis, Minneapolis, and 236 other populated locations.

The army conceded that it had released microorganisms at Washington National Airport in 1965 and into the New York City subway system in 1966 during peak travel hours. The purpose of this little experiment was to see how the bacteria spread and survived as people went about their daily routines. The army still sprays bacteria outdoors at Dugway Proving Ground, just 70 miles from Salt Lake City.

Though declaring that bacteria no longer are being disseminated over American cities, the army admits that as recently as the 1980s it conducted more than 170 open-air tests at Dugway. The stated purpose was to evaluate the performance of biological-detector systems.

Many Utah residents remember that when a nerve-gas agent was released in 1968, it killed 6,000 sheep 20 miles away. Yet the army has failed to acknowledge that such microorganisms can reproduce quickly and be efficiently transported by winds. It euphemistically refers to the bacteria as harmless "simulant materials."

This response has not satisfied Utah officials, scientists, and medical experts. As early as 1950 there were indications that the army's experiments might be causing harm. That same year San Francisco was blanketed with bacteria sprayed from an offshore boat. Within days, hospital patients began to develop heart and urinary-tract infections, causing at least one patient to die.

The army still officially considers its test bacteria harmless, and no one knows the full extent of the effects. Nasty rumors abound as a result of the secrecy surrounding the biological defense program. The most recent involves the hanta virus, the apparent cause of a number of headline-making fatalities. It had been studied by military researchers for years, and speculation has arisen that the virus may have been connected to the outbreak.

Suspicions could be reduced if this program were under civilian jurisdiction and open to scrutiny. A 1989 army document claimed that all biological defense work is now unclassified. But in typical military doublespeak, it also stated that the results of that work may, in fact, be classified.

The army still neglects to monitor the health of citizens who may be exposed during its tests. And it still insists that its bacterial agents cause no harm. Meanwhile, the human guinea pigs in these frightening experiments remain uninformed and unconsenting.

HUMAN RADIATION TESTS

In December 1993, the U.S. government began a sweeping investigation of secret radiation experiments that had been conducted from the 1940s until the early 1970s. Energy Secretary Hazel O'Leary reported being "heartsick" when she learned that some of the studies done by the old Atomic Energy Commission (AEC) recruited subjects who had no idea they were being used as guinea pigs. O'Leary told *Newsweek*: "Who were these people conducting experiments, and why did this happen? The only thing I could think of was Nazi Germany."

In 1986, a congressional subcommittee chaired by Rep. Edward Markey, D-Mass., uncovered many of these same facts in a report entitled "American Nuclear Guinea Pigs." Markey reported that U.S. citizens "became nuclear calibration devices for experimenters run amok . . . Too many of these experiments used human subjects that were captive audiences or populations considered expendable: the elderly, prisoners, hospital patients who might not have retained their full faculties for informed consent."

More than 800 people were exposed to radiation in these government tests, and many were apparently unaware of the risks they were taking. The following are some of the experiments that came to light:

- As part of the Manhattan Project that developed the atom bomb, five persons were identified as among 18 hospital patients who were given "tracer" injections of plutonium. The purpose of this 1940s experiment was to determine what radiation doses government workers might be exposed to safely. Plutonium, we now know, happens to be one of the most toxic substances in existence. In 1993 the *Albuquerque Tribune* reported a case involving an impoverished railroad porter from Texas who had plutonium injected into his injured leg. Three days later the leg was amputated above the knee and carried away by researchers.

- As many as 125 mentally retarded children ate or were injected with radioactive material in studies at Fernald State School in Waltham, Massachusetts. The students thought they were part of a "science club." A letter to parents made no mention of radiation, stating only that the children would be given a special diet to study the way the body absorbs cereals, iron, and vitamins.

- In a 1948 study, several hundred women at a prenatal clinic at Vanderbilt University were given iron pills bombarded with radiation. At Boston's Lying-In Hospital 23 pregnant women were injected with radioactive iron during a blood study of pregnant women and their infants. Today, expectant mothers are strongly urged to avoid all radiation exposure.

- According to the General Accounting Office, radiation was deliberately released into the atmosphere in at least a dozen secret tests between 1948 and 1952 in New Mexico, Tennessee, and Utah. This was part of a program to develop a radiological weapon or defend against one in the event the Soviets developed a "death spray." At the same time, the Hanford facility in Washington released a huge cloud of radioactive iodine to see how far downwind it could be traced.

- Beginning in 1963, 131 inmates at two prisons in Oregon and Washington were used in AEC experiments. These men agreed to submit to X-ray radiation of their scrotum and testes. They were warned about the chance of sterility and radiation burns, but not about the risk of testicular cancer.

- In 1964, NASA and the AEC began researching the risks astronauts would face from radiation exposure in space. They built special labs at Oak Ridge, Tennessee, placing radioactive cobalt and cesium in the walls and brought in some 200 patients from civilian hospitals, many of them with cancer. One official called the room "virtually a sea of radiation."

Scientists from the early days of the nuclear age defend the validity of many of these tests. "We should be cautious about criticizing their work," retired astrophysicist John Simpson told *Newsweek*. "If research had not been done on humans, radioactive dangers would be greater throughout the world today."

Other scientists pointed out that most of the experiments involved very low levels of radiation. Edward Teller, the developer of the hydrogen bomb, said, "I think that human experiments without the consent of the people is wrong." But he added, "I also believe the actual damage that has been done has been greatly exaggerated."

What the real truth is, only time will tell.

NOTES

1. James E. Jones, *Bad Blood: The Tuskegee Syphilis Experiment*, New York: The Free Press (1981 and 1993): 10-11.

Chapter 5

BODIES FOR RENT: SURROGATE PARENTHOOD

WANTED: SURROGATE MOTHERS
CARRY A CHILD FOR AN INFERTILE COUPLE.
Tubal ligation OK.
Egg donors needed.
Mothers only.
Call attorney at 1-800-696-4664.

Since the late 1970s, there has been a new wave of baby making. In the United States and Canada, there are an estimated 4.9 million childless couples with infertility problems, and some of them are choosing surrogacy (other women carrying their children) to make their dream of parenthood a reality. Some women are born without uteruses or suffer other abnormalities that make childbearing impossible. Some are rendered infertile as a result of pelvic inflammatory disease. In a minority of cases, chronic ill health makes pregnancy inadvisable. And then, of course, there are a significant number of men who have a low or impaired sperm count. When these problems do not respond to medical treatment, surrogacy becomes an option.

There are several different types of surrogacy. Type one is the traditional form: the surrogate is inseminated with the male partner's sperm.

Type two is in-vitro fertilization (IVF) surrogacy, legally known as gestational carrier. This involves the transfer of one or more embryos derived from the gametes (eggs and sperm) of both members of the infertile couple to the uterus of the third party (the surrogate). With IVF surrogacy, the surrogate provides a host womb. For women under the age of 39, payment can range from around $14,000 to $24,000, to cover three IVF embryo transplant attempts, medications, and donor and agency fees for a period of 12 months to two years.

If you are a woman who is having difficulty conceiving, there are women who are more than willing to carry your child. In the United States there are more than 100 fertility centers and centers for surrogate parenting. A woman who "rents" her womb can make around $12,500 for a 40-week pregnancy. When one considers that pregnancy is a 24-hour a day job, the fee averages out to about $1.80 an hour. Sometimes a clothing allowance of up to $500 is paid by the center, as well as travel expenses.

EGGS FOR SALE

The average woman is born with approximately 480 to 600 eggs in her ovaries. And just one of these eggs can be sold for as much as $3,000. But harvesting them is not an easy process: the eggs must be surgically removed, which requires an abdominal incision. Although I've been told it's not too painful, any entry into the abdominal cavity can produce infection and other complications. Any woman considering becoming a donor should carefully consider the risks and discuss them with her physician.

To research this subject, I spoke with Melinda Moore, age 32, from Chowchilla, California. Already a parent of two, Melinda wanted very much to become a surrogate mother. She believes that every couple should be able to have a child, and she wanted to take part in helping people with fertility problems.

She first called an adoption agency, which suggested she contact the Beverly Hills Center for Surrogate Parenting. For the first month Melinda had to go though a psychological profile study. This was followed by long days of medical testing and then more tests to determine the size of her eggs and the timing of her ovulations. Finally, she was told that she was qualified and was, in fact, the perfect donor candidate.

Melinda signed on for the program, became impregnated, and for nine months stayed on a careful diet, took her vitamins, and made long monthly trips to her doctor in Sacramento.

When her labor began, Melinda notified the surrogate parents, who rushed to the hospital. When her beautiful child was born, Melinda shed tears of happiness for the joy she was giving to the formerly childless couple.

Melinda was paid $500 for a maternity wardrobe and other items, and she received a fee of $10,000. She remains in close contact with the new parents, and every holiday they send gifts to Melinda's children.

Melinda's story is a best-case scenario. Recent headlines have announced cases where birth mothers have tried—and in some cases succeeded—in reclaiming their children from their adoptive parents. The risk of such legal proceedings always exists, so adoptive parents should work with a reputable agency that carefully screens prospective surrogate mothers-to-be. And those wishing to become surrogates should be certain of their motives and not enter into such an arrangement if they feel even the slightest ambivalence.

UTERUS FOR RENT

Being a surrogate mother was also a dream of Victoria Leeyers of San Diego. She finalized this dream in August 1993 after giving birth to an infertile couple's first genetic child. At the time she was told she was one of about 200 women being a gestational carrier. This means it was completely the other couple's egg and sperm.

Victoria was a true believer in surrogacy and felt it should be expanded into San Diego County. She used her experience and skills as a former business owner to help her form Surrogate Parenting Connection in November 1993. "I believe the reason why a surrogate becomes a surrogate is because she wants to see the joy in the couple's eyes when she delivers the child," she says. Victoria's agency pays $14,000 to $15,000 to the surrogate. She also maintains a close relationship with the new parents.

WE NEED YOUR SPERM

Unlike women who are born with only so many eggs at birth, men make millions of sperm cells every day. Maybe that's why they don't get paid as much as women do for their donations.

Almost every large city has two or three sperm banks, and infertility centers can be found almost everywhere. Not everyone can sell sperm, and you may not want to after finding out how much work you must go through. First, you must undergo a lot of testing and paperwork, determine your sperm count, and have no sex for up to three days. Then, if you are accepted, you masturbate and then ejaculate in a tub. You receive no cream so you must ejaculate dry—though some places will give you a *Playboy* to look at. The pay is about $45 to $65 per specimen in most cases. Just look in your phone book under Infertility, or watch for ads in the paper searching for couples with infertility problems. If they're looking for women, they're also looking for men. You can also check with your local hospital.

SUPER SPERM—ONLY THE BEST

Calling all Nobel Prize winners! Doctors, lawyers, scientists, professors, or anyone else with special qualities. The Repository for Germinal Choice in Escondido, California, is looking for you—and in most cases will find you.

This nonprofit organization is dedicated to collecting sperm from "outstandingly intelligent and healthy men"; the sperm is then frozen and made available to couples who cannot have children because of the husbands' infertility. Couples may choose which of the sperm donors they prefer to become the biological father of their children. The couples are given detailed information about the traits of the donors, but not the names.

Do you meet the profile of a suitable donor? This is the profile of one typical donor:

ANCESTRY: Austrian
EYE COLOR: Blue-green
SKIN: Fair
HAIR: Golden blond, naturally curly
HEIGHT: 6' 4"
APPEARANCE: Very handsome, superb
    physique
BORN: Late 1960s
IQ: 142 on Binet scale
HOBBIES: Member of an Olympic swim-
    ming team; genetic research; writing
BLOOD TYPE: A-

Among hundreds of sperm banks in the United States, there are only a few that screen donors for intelligence. Prices won't be discussed over the phone, but you can assume that they will buy your sperm for around $200 to $300, and if you need to buy sperm, three vials cost about $3,000.

The results are hard to judge because of privacy, but of 150 children born so far to families using this service, all were said to be "bright and healthy," and those in school were reportedly doing well.

Chapter 6

BAD BLOOD, GOOD BLOOD

Blood is the source of life. It is always needed on a worldwide basis, both for research and to save lives.

Examination of the blood is where most medical testing begins, for it is the destination of everything we eat, drink, or inhale. Consequently, there are many labs and plasma centers out there competing for blood donors. Many people who live on the street or at the poverty level will end up at a local plasma center. Two hours of one's time will bring in $15 to $20 up to twice a week. The appeal to those in financial straits is obvious.

But if you don't need the money, the blood banks will be more than happy to take your blood for free. You do get a complimentary AIDS test, plus donuts and coffee or juice. You also may receive a free T-shirt.

In many cases, your blood may be given to a family member or friend in need. But did you know that the blood that you donate—whole blood and components— can be sold for about $214 by your local blood bank? These centers say they need about 400 donors a day. The blood they receive is sold on consignment to hospitals and research laboratories. In most cases, the price will not be charged until the blood is transfused.

Body for Sale

56

Blood: The Universal Lifeline

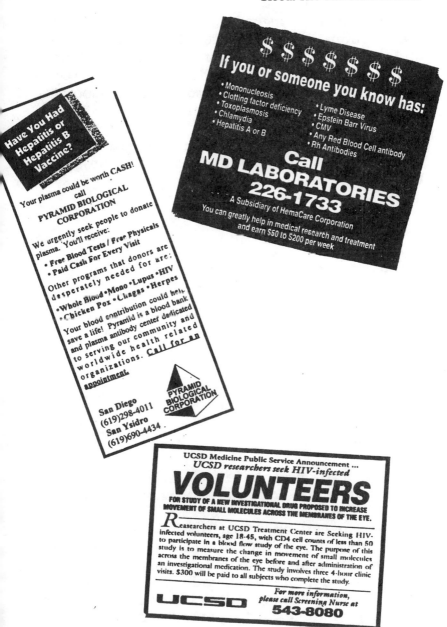

THE "BEST" OF BLOOD

If your blood happens to be unique, you have some other options. Research labs are looking for infected and rare types of blood. Do you have hepatitis, Rh negative blood, AIDS, or some kind of unusual blood condition? If so, your blood can be sold at many laboratories and research centers at a price of $50 to $200 for each donation.

There are other programs where donors are desperately needed. Whole blood and blood from those with the following conditions are in demand:

- Mononucleosis
- Lupus
- HIV
- Chicken pox
- Chagas
- Epstein-Barr virus
- Low T-cell counts
- Toxoplasmosi
- CMV
- Rh antibodies
- Chlamydia
- Lyme disease
- Clotting factor deficiency
- Herpes

Check in you local phone book under blood bank or biological research, or look for research studies on blood in your local papers.

Even the National Institutes of Health has a Platelets Center at its Clinical Center Department of Transfusion Medicine in Bethesda, where virtually every component of blood is needed. Platelets are small cells that circulate in the blood stream and help produce clotting when necessary. They are manufactured in bone marrow and may be stored in the spleen.

CRYING WOLF

We have all seen headlines and articles about critical shortages at local blood banks. This is sometimes true, but often such statements are merely public relations strategies to beef up donations. The reasons for the low supply vary from freezing temperatures to violence in the streets to major accidents on holidays to natural disasters. Although some of these situations are valid causes for a dwindling blood supply, sometimes the case is intentionally overstated in order to encourage free donations. Alerting the public to a critical shortage gets people moving. Plasma centers provide competition for the blood banks; they too are desperately seeking donors and are better able to pay them. All this makes for a competitive market and fosters a do-whatever-is-necessary mentality.

WHERE TO SELL "BAD" BLOOD

Many San Diego, Los Angeles, New York, and San Francisco newspapers run ads seeking HIV or AIDS patients and those with a T-cell count below 200. Some studies pay up to $1,000 for blood donations. In Los Angeles, you can call (818) 906-6279.

Essential Biologics, Inc. in San Diego and Los Angeles needs volunteers to participate in a clotting factor deficiency program and will pay from $200–300 per week. They are also looking for O-negative mothers and will pay $300 per month in San Diego. Call (619) 682-5252.

HemaCare Corporation is a national company looking for blood. Check your local phone directory for its number.

MAN'S BEST FRIEND IS ALSO
LOOKING FOR BLOOD

With all the publicity about the supply and demand for human blood, there is now a veterinary blood bank, so if you've got a healthy dog, it can also donate blood to save your neighbor's poodle. A new TV public service announcement features Pepe, a little Chihuahua whose life was saved by Max, a German shepherd. The film announcement was made for the Eastern Veterinary Blood Bank.

BLOOD FROM THE DEAD

Do you think that blood from a dead body could be worth anything? From 1930 to 1960, the Sklifosovsky Institute in Russia transfused more than 50,000 pints of cadaver blood. The Russians found that, if it is drained within six hours, blood from these bodies can be used in many instances. Using cadaver blood has also been studied in the United States and in the Ukraine. Some feel that the use of cadaver blood could help reduce the chronic shortages of safe blood for transfusions.[1]

NOTES

1. Kenneth V. Iverson, M.D., *Death to Dust* (Tucson: Galen Press): 69.

Chapter 7

Experts say that the human body can be worth up to a million dollars. What, then, would Albert Einstein's brain be worth? Or Thomas Edison's? Most of us don't have that million-dollar brain, but our bodies, when broken down into precious parts, are a valuable commodity.

So what is a human body really worth? Prices vary throughout the world. In some places it can be worth its weight in gold, whereas in others it may be worth only two cents. Laws differ from country to country and state to state, and the rules are constantly changing. With a growing demand for a longer life, some people are willing to pay almost anything to buy themselves a few extra years. For example, if a man doesn't want to die of kidney failure, he may be willing to spend $20,000 to purchase a new kidney.

MARKET PRICE LIST

CORNEAS	$900 to $16,000
HEART	$2,000 to $25,000
BONE MARROW	$25 to $7,000
MEN'S SPERM	$35 to $100
WOMEN'S EGGS	$2,000 to $2,500
KIDNEY	$1,000 to $30,000

BODY PARTS THAT CAN BE USED ONE MORE TIME

This is a list of spare body parts that are currently transplanted into needy recipients. With today's medical advances, almost every body part that is preserved within minutes after death can be reused one more time. Below is a list of the parts most in need.

TO GIVE OR SELL?

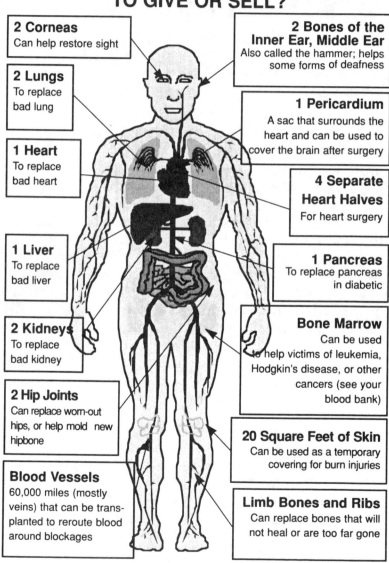

2 Corneas
Can help restore sight

2 Lungs
To replace
bad lung

1 Heart
To replace
bad heart

1 Liver
To replace
bad liver

2 Kidneys
To replace
bad kidney

2 Hip Joints
Can replace worn-out hips, or help mold new hipbone

Blood Vessels
60,000 miles (mostly veins) that can be transplanted to reroute blood around blockages

2 Bones of the Inner Ear, Middle Ear
Also called the hammer; helps some forms of deafness

1 Pericardium
A sac that surrounds the heart and can be used to cover the brain after surgery

4 Separate Heart Halves
For heart surgery

1 Pancreas
To replace pancreas in diabetic

Bone Marrow
Can be used to help victims of leukemia, Hodgkin's disease, or other cancers (see your blood bank)

20 Square Feet of Skin
Can be used as a temporary covering for burn injuries

Limb Bones and Ribs
Can replace bones that will not heal or are too far gone

LUNG	$1,000 to $12,000
BLOOD	$20 to $230
PLASMA	$15 to $60

STANDING IN LINE IN INDIA

India's profound poverty provides great incentive for its citizens to trade body parts for a chance at a better life. As of 1996, the selling of body parts became legal in Madras and Bombay. With a population of more than 500 million and a high death rate, it's no wonder people are standing in line at the local hospitals ready, willing, and able to sell one of their parts.

All who take part in this must be tested to see if they are a viable match for someone in need of a new organ. The going price at this time for a kidney is about 60,000 rupees, equivalent to US$1,000. A heart can bring in as much as $5,000 if it is removed quickly and is accessible for a hasty transplant. When Indian citizens started flocking to the hospitals wanting to sell their eyes, the government said it would consider putting limits on which organs could be marketed. One newspaper article in Calcutta reported the following:

> CALCUTTA—Six hospital orderlies made more than $240,000 in five years by plucking the eyes out of dead and dying patients and selling them to eye banks!

CHINESE EXECUTIONS FOR BODY PARTS

A recent report from China attests to extreme measures for procuring organs:

> BEIJING—According to the Associated Press, executed prisoners are the source of most organ transplants in China, and the donors sometimes are still alive when their organs are removed. Executions seem to be scheduled according to transplant needs,

according to Human Rights Watch—Asia in an August 1994 report. In some cases executions were deliberately botched to keep the bodies alive longer and improve chances of organ transplant success. The group said that prisoners' consent was rarely sought, or is coerced in the last few hours before death.

KIDNAPPING CHILDREN FOR SPARE PARTS

Recent mob attacks in Guatemala on two U.S. women suspected of kidnapping children for organ transplants may be part of a Guatemalan right-wing strategy to create a climate of instability hostile to human-rights monitors. In the more serious of the two incidents, June D. Weinstock, an environmental writer from Fairbanks, Alaska, was engulfed by an enraged mob in San Cristobal Verapas, in the Mayan highlands, after she was seen caressing a child whose mother reported him missing immediately afterward. Weinstock was stripped, stoned, stabbed repeatedly, and beaten unconscious by her assailants, who were egged on by state workers and unidentified outsiders.

Weinstock currently resides in Alaska and, according to reports, has not fully recovered from her brutal attack. But she insists that she was in no way connected with the selling of children's body parts.

But there are reports that this horrific practice may indeed take place. In March 1994, Mexico's *Proceso*, which has been tracking baby-trafficking for international adoptions, interviewed Eric Sottas, president of the Geneva-based World Organization against Torture, who confirmed the existence of international rings that kidnap children, "not only for illegal adoptions, pornographic activities, and child prostitution, but for the purpose of 'trafficking in organs.'"

The "Sollas Report," written over a three-year period with the collaboration of 200 human-rights agencies, was presented 8 March 1994 at a conference of transplant experts in Basel, Switzerland. Among other horrors, the report listed 17 clinics in Tijuana and Juarez, on Mexico's U.S. border, that perform sophisticated transplants of kidneys and corneal tissues from kidnapped children to wealthy Europeans and North Americans who pay top prices for the operations—no questions asked. The Latin American countries listed as confirmed traffickers in child organs are Brazil, Argentina, Peru, Honduras, Colombia, and Mexico. The chief beneficiaries, apart from North Americans, are reported to be Swiss, German, and Italian buyers.

In an earlier report to the United Nations, Sottas named Guatemala, Haiti, and Brazil as three countries in which street children are kidnapped for their organs. Most of these children are never heard from again. The baby trade is so lucrative that high government officials are said to take part in it—illegal adoptions can bring as much as $10,000.

Meanwhile, the stories of child abduction for illicit purposes continue to proliferate throughout Latin America. The *Los Angeles Times* reported in its 1 May 1994 edition the following:

> LOS ANGELES—In Guatemala, the organ-trafficking rumors refuse to go away. Even if these claims continue to elude confirmation, the verifiable story of a Guatemalan Supreme Court president who heads a child trafficking ring is sinister enough to cause stupor in Washington and European capitals, and to keep the pot boiling within Guatemala. As long as army generals and high-level officials continue to get away with systematic assassinations and infant abductions, the chances are slim that a U.N.-sponsored truth commission could get the job done, and pin down those responsible for the murder and disappearance of more that 100,000 Guatemalans in one of the hemisphere's bloodiest and longest-lasting armed conflicts.

COMPLEX ETHICS

In the United States, the idea of organs for sale—under any conditions—is considered so grisly that the purchase or sale of human organs was outlawed by federal legislation in 1984. But as the following editorial from the *San Diego Union-Tribune*, 31 August 1992, asks, is this is the wisest course?

SAN DIEGO—[Selling body parts] violates the sanctity of the human body and collides with the most basic precept of medicine: do no harm. The U.S. transplant system relies on voluntary donations, from live relatives and dead donors—mainly highway-accident victims. However . . . many people die for lack of transplantable organs, even as transplant techniques become ever safer and more promising.

With worthy people dying who might otherwise be saved, the question must be asked: Since almost everything else is for sale, why not a market in healthy human kidneys and other organs that can be spared, taken from cash-hungry donors for transplanting into patients with ready cash?

Indeed, why not? As in India and other Third World countries with centers of high-tech medicine, the booming trade in kidney transplants benefits wealthy patients and provides several thousand dollars for each donor. In the wealthy West, that may look like blood money. But it is an otherwise unattainable fortune in countries where per-capita incomes are only a few hundred dollars a year.

Daniel Greenberg, Washington columnist for the *San Diego Union-Tribune*, points out that by providing the purchase price for a business or a farm, the proceeds from the sale of a kidney can free a Third World family from unrelenting poverty, and the donor can still live a long, healthy life. Viewed in the harsh context of Third World deprivation, the kidney market is arguably not a bad deal.

Did you know?

Nationwide there are approximately 39,317 people waiting.

25,428 people awaiting a kidney transplant

5,000 people needing corneal transplants

3,253 people awaiting a liver transplant

2,904 people awaiting a heart transplant

972 people in need of a kidney/pancreas transplant

200 people in need of a pancreas transplant

203 people awaiting heart-lung transplants

1,309 people needing lung transplants

48 people needing intestines *

Plus, there are thousands who are in need of skin grafts, heart valve replacements, bone transplants and other tissue grafts. Last year the Northwest Organ Procurement Agency reported recovering 169 kidneys, 43 hearts, 69 livers, 20 lungs, and 37 pancreata.

Yet, approximately *one-third* of the people needing organ transplants will die for want of an organ.

Over 78%[1] of those responding to a survey say that organ donation has a positive effect on the donor family's grieving process.

[1]Batten & Prottas(1978)
*Source: United Network for Organ Sharing, March 8, 1994

WAITING FOR LIFE—OR DEATH

Organ donation from live donors seems to make sense in developed as well as in Third World nations. In the United States alone, more than 33,400 patients are registered on the Organ Procurement and Transplant Network awaiting a donor, and the number increases by approximately 1,000 each month.

Though the costs of transplants are high—generally from $40,000 to $250,000 —transplantation ultimately saves money. For example, kidney transplants cost approximately $50,000. But over six years, the procedure, including the high cost of immunosuppressive medications, can save $85,000 in medical costs of dialysis (a process for cleansing the blood of toxins by an artificial kidney machine) and related medical treatments.

Since December 1988 the number of people waiting for a kidney has increased 80 percent; for a heart, 174 percent; and for a liver, 394 percent. Successful organ transplants have increased since the advent of the immunosuppressive drug Cyclosporine—from 7,731 in 1984 to more than 18,000 in 1993. Twice that number of patients could have received transplants if there had been more organ donors.

In 1993 approximately 3,000 people died waiting for a transplant because organs were not available. About 150,000 Americans suffer from chronic kidney failure and need dialysis or kidney transplantation to stay alive. Approximately 20 percent of patients waiting for a liver transplant are under 18 years of age. Before 1980, fewer than 100 heart transplants were performed annually. In 1993, 2,290 were performed at 164 centers. The one-year survival rate for heart transplants is now 77 percent.

The criteria for patient selection for a transplant are time on the waiting list, medical urgency, and blood type—not necessarily in that order. In the case of kidneys, tissue match is also a factor. All potential donors (living and cadaver) are tested for infectious diseases (including HIV) before being accepted as donors. The average age of organ recipients is 39 for kidneys, 45 for hearts, 32 for heart-lungs, 36 for livers, 43 for lungs, and 35 for pancreas.

With the technology available to save lives and the need so profound, perhaps it's time we reevaluate our ethics regarding the voluntary sale of our organs. As Greenberg poignantly states, "In the U.S. we consider such a notion . . . so grisly that the purchase or sale of human organs was outlawed in 1984. However, the yield from the donor system remains inadequate to the need by a wide mark."

At a time when transplant techniques have become incredibly sophisticated and capable of extending life, people are forced to wait and hope for the kindness of strangers. And all too often they wait in vain.

The United Network for Organ Sharing reports that in 1991, there were 39,872 candidates for transplants in the United States, but only enough organs to provide for 16,025. Another 2,518 persons died while waiting. In the case of cadavers, 4,534 organs were collected, but this was only a small increase from previous years.

Greenberg suggests that one way to acquire more organs within the present cultural bounds is to provide a small financial incentive for persons authorizing after-death renewal of their organs for transplanting. Since outright sale of organs collides with too many cultural sensitivities, Greenberg suggests that benefits go only to the heirs of the dead organ donor and to the patients faced with an otherwise fatal illness.

"Would more people sign the donor card in return for a minor enhancement of their legacy?" asks Greenberg. "It's worth a try."[1]

NOTES

1. Daniel Greenberg, "Body parts for sale—Financial incentives now could assure greater supply of transplant organs," *San Diego Union-Tribune* (31 August 1992): B-5.

Chapter 8

CADAVERS FOR CASH: WHAT HAPPENS AT THE MORGUE

Not only has Western society cringed at the idea of individuals marketing their organs, it has been equally reluctant to tolerate research on or organ harvesting from cadavers. In the past the practice has only been allowed when it appears to significantly advance medical science, but now the situation is changing.

In Heidelberg, West Germany, dead bodies of men, women, and children have recently been used in testing car crashes in place of the traditional dummies. Members of the cadavers' families received compensation, and those bodies that were unclaimed by survivors were "donated." In some of the tests, corpses are strapped into cars that collide with other vehicles, walls, and various barriers to measure the impact on the human body. Are the Germans trying to make a better Volkswagen?

When the German public discovered this practice, they responded with more than a little outrage, and, for the moment, the practice has been put on hold. "In an age when experiments on animals are in question, such tests must be carried out on dummies and not on children's cadavers," asserted Germany's largest automobile club, ADAC.

The Germans are not alone in testing corpses in automobile pileups. The French car company, Renault, is said to have made use of some 450 bodies in accident simulations.

In the United States, cadaver research has been practiced to some extent for decades. George Parker, an associate administrator for the National Highway Traffic Safety Administration (NHTSA), stated that such research studies are absolutely essential for motor vehicle safety. The NHTSA also funds $2.5 million each year for cadaver collision research—however, only adult bodies are used in these tests.

Most of us try to live life to the fullest while we can, because we know our bodies will not go on forever. Now, as we approach a new century, things are changing. Many of our body parts can remain on this earth, while (it is hoped) our souls move on.

As death approaches, we are concerned with remembrances of a lifetime of precious experiences or perhaps with the possibility of life after death. On a more immediate level, there is the question of our will: who gets what and how family and loved ones will be provided for. Only rarely do we think about what might happen to the body we leave behind.

FROM HERE TO ETERNITY

Your final scenario might go something like this: You feel like an elephant has just stepped on your chest. You can't believe the incredible pain you are experiencing. You have a sinking feeling that something is very, very wrong. All of a sudden your heart gives out, you fall to the floor, the room goes dark. What do your loved ones do? Whom do they call? The "Morgue Busters," of course. They arrive and pronounce you dead. Then, the big wagon comes to take you for your last ride.

Where do they take you? The morgue. And while you're on ice or in the cooler, the morgue releases your

phone number to a donation center or research foundation; then they call your closest family member to determine how to dispose of your body. But they risk getting a
busy signal, because the donation center may be also
hastily dialing your immediate family.

This is an example of such a call:

> Hi, my name is Fred S. from the City Eye Bank.
> We're so sorry about the death of your loved one and
> offer you our deepest sympathy. We are calling today
> to find out if you would like to donate a cornea from the
> eye of the deceased?
>
> You can be assured that your dear one will still look
> good for the viewing. But you only have about four
> hours to let us know because time is of the essence.
> Can you please call me back as soon as possible?

Imagine how this call might affect your family
members, who are still not over the shock of your
death! But this is reality. The donation centers must
move quickly, for they only have a brief window of time
to work within. So you must look at the situation objec-
tively. Your life as you once knew it is over, but it may
be just the beginning for someone else who is waiting
for your precious parts.

The Gift of Sight
Is the precious gift of sight really free? No. This is what
happens when an individual is given a second chance at
seeing the world. The county coroner calls the eye bank
to inform it that there has been a body donation. The eye
bank then hires a surgeon at an average fee of $900 to
extract the two corneas and package them on ice.

The eye bank has a freezer full of corneas just waiting
for a doctor's call, searching for a cornea of a certain
size and shape. A $2,000 "transfer fee" is set by the eye
bank, and the transplant doctor receives the cornea—on

ice—by overnight express. The doctor then sells his time and the cornea to the patient for a fee that ranges from $16,000 to $24,000.

A Trip to the Morgue

A day at the medical examiner's office, behind the scenes . . . it all takes place behind the wooden doors. The body ends up here.

In a normal 24-hour period, anywhere from four to 14 bodies arrive here so that experts can determine the cause of death. About 50 percent of deaths occur in hospitals or in situations where the cause of death is known. But for those who end up here, behind the doors, the rips and cuts begin, and soon the official cause of death will be certified.

At this point, the researchers—or the "transplanters" as the medical examiner (ME) prefers to call them—are notified. Many people have organ donor IDs on the front of their drivers' licenses that inform the hospital or ME of their wishes. Others choose to go straight to their resting place. But if no one comes to claim the body, there are "body snatchers" just waiting. The "transplanters" will arrive within 12 hours to claim the body parts they want: eyes (corneas), skin, bones, and joints. Kidneys and other bloodpumping parts usually are removed in the hospital. After the parts are removed and the body sewn up, it is then shipped off to the cemetery for a well-deserved rest in peace.

THINK BEFORE YOU GIVE!

Although donating body parts and organs is certainly a noble gesture, you may want to think for a moment before signing any documents. Do you want your body parts to be given to someone on a waiting list, or would you prefer to see them sold and have your heirs receive payment for your kidneys, hearts, lungs, or corneas?

In the United States, there are only a few states that will allow you to sell your body whole or in part before you are dead. If you happen to know of someone who is in need of your heart or kidneys and you do not wish to give yours away, you can make arrangements through an attorney to sell them and have the money go to your family.

Many states like California put a red dot on your driver's license to signify that you're giving the gift of life, and, when you die, your body parts may be donated to research institutions, hospitals, or living banks.

On New Year's Day 1986, a new state law was passed in California that had a special significance for surgeons, nurses, and specialists involved with organ donations. This law *requires* hospitals to approach families or representatives of deceased patients about the possibility of donating the victim's body parts, tissue, organs, or bones to an organ-procurement agency.

There are concerns now that the new agencies will be competing for the limited supply of donor organs from brain-dead patients or tissue and bone from cadavers.

GOING FOR THE GOLD

Many people are laid to rest in the ground with a nice tombstone on top. It's one of the most expensive ways to go. As the times change, more and more people ask to be cremated. It's fast and cheap and saves space. When the body is put in the heat incinerator, it then will become ashes (about nine pounds worth).

Most of us don't think of the gold that's still in our mouth. Gold does not burn but will melt. Gold will come to rest at the bottom of the incinerator in one spot. There have been cases documented where morticians pocket the gold. With the current going price for gold about $380, this can amount to a pretty penny. Make arrangements to have yours go to the person of your choice or to collect that of loved ones.

ILLEGAL HARVESTING OF BODY PARTS

Many people are unaware that some members of the funeral industry and medical and transplantation organizations engage in illegal harvesting of body parts.

In Pasadena, California, there was a case where morticians were making a profit selling body parts in funeral parlors and crematoriums. Heads sold for $85, corneas went for $565, and kidneys and spleens brought in up to $300. Medical schools were buying more than half of the body parts. Thomas Frankovich, an attorney who represented more than 100 families suing the funeral home, said that the owners were facing 67 criminal counts, including multiple cremation of human remains and mixing decedent ashes, as well as unlawful removal of body parts and harvesting gold and silver from cadavers.

At the University of California in San Diego (UCSD), a sworn affidavit told of the possible illegal sale of body parts. A 24-page affidavit was filed in court, detailing how bodies and parts of bodies allegedly were removed from UCSD Medical Center and other hospitals around the county. Reports alleged that the sale involved at least $17,000 worth of bone procured from cadavers.

In still another incident, a physician who serves as medical director for a private tissue bank may have been involved in possible illegal harvesting or obtaining of body parts from at least 10 cadavers and may be involved in "criminal activity." The evidence in the affidavit successfully supported search warrants of the San Diego Regional Tissue Bank, Alva Professional Services, and Professional Mortuary Services, all of San Diego. The evidence obtained after a search included numerous files and records, and bags of human bone tissue.

In the sworn affidavit, which was completely unsealed by Municipal Court Judge Exarhos at the request of the *San Diego Union* newspaper, the following was obtained by university police officer Robert L. Jones an hour after Jonathan Leroy McIntyre, owner and operator of the San Diego Regional Tissue Bank, officially resigned his position at UCSD Medical Center. He removed—without authorization—the body of an elderly man from UCSD's morgue. Records stated that the man's family had not authorized the donation of tissue or bone. Unfortunately, the affidavit did not say if the body was ever recovered.

Also, the body of a deceased woman, which had been donated to the UCSD School of Medicine for use as a teaching device, possibly had bone harvested without authorization while it was stored at Professional Mortuary Services. It is interesting to note that, according to university officials, the operation rendered the body useless for either teaching or research.

McIntyre admitted "having harvested the bone," according to statements by John Sykes, curator at the School of Medicine at that time. McIntyre returned most, but not all, of the leg bones, but none of the ear bones, according to the affidavit.

UCSD donor records on a young girl who died at the hospital were "taken, and file numbers on the other donor files were changed to cover up the missing file," officials said, according to the affidavit. Although UCSD had no record of the removal of any of the girl's bones, a coroner's autopsy confirmed that bone had indeed been harvested from the hip and ankles.

Medical Arts Hospital, a 71-bed for-profit facility in Dallas, Texas, paid for and received $11,790 worth of human bone from Alva Professional Services, according to bank records. Alva was not and is not approved as a laboratory to harvest bone, according to officials of the California Health Department, which licenses labs for this type of work. Lawrence Alva "Lee" Dyer, who owned Alva at the time and who has also contracted with UCSD to transport cadavers since 1984, was seeking state approval to operate a firm called Organ Donation Centre, which would route organs to individuals.

Records show that McIntyre's San Diego Regional Tissue Bank received a $5,250 check from Medical Arts Hospital the day the tissue bank was approved by California to harvest bone. The affidavit states that San Diego Regional had billed Medical Arts the $5,250 for "thirty-five bone plugs at a unit price of $150." (Bone plugs are commonly used in spinal surgery, and a special drill press is used on cadavers to produce a plug.)

RUSSIAN BONES FOR SALE

The fall of the Iron Curtain produced a trade that no one wants—international brokers selling tissue from a "butcher's list" of body parts taken from people potentially infected with viral diseases.

In February 1995, the *San Diego Union-Tribune* reported that the San Diego Tissue Bank had widely distributed human bone imported from Russia that was not adequately inspected for infectious agents.[1] The FDA used new emergency regulations to recall and destroy the questionable bone, but it was learned that much of the bone had already been implanted in patients.

Allo Tech, an El Paso firm, was said to have imported at least 188 half-skeletons, which were then cut into hundreds of pieces. Authorities said Allo Tech paid about $5,000 per half-skeleton, then marked up the processed bone so that each skeleton could bring tens of thousands of dollars in revenue.

According to the *Union-Tribune*, a half-skeleton produces a variety of tissue pieces used in reconstructive surgery. A lilac crest (worth $1,500) can be cut into blocks, plugs, and dowels for spinal-fusion surgery. A patella (kneecap) ligament is worth about $1,000, an Achilles tendon $700, a tibia $600, a femur $300, and a fibula $250.

It's illegal to sell tissue or bone, but tissue banks can charge fees to recover costs, moving the money through nonprofit and for-profit companies. It becomes hard to draw the line between costs and profits.

THE DOOR TO DEATH

As part of my research for this book, I decided to make a visit to the Cadaver Department at the UCSD School of Medicine. I trust it will be my last. A cold feeling went through me as I walked down the hall on the basement floor. I knew I was nearing the "door of death." I stopped, turned, and noticed that there was nobody around; I realized that everyone was out to lunch.

The door was half open, and I couldn't resist walking inside. In that unforgettable room I saw lined up on approximately 12 metal shelves—stacked from floor to ceiling—literally dozens of dead bodies. To my right were 15 tables, each with a tray. On top of the trays lay various body parts. It was a sight that is usually seen only by interns and students in the medical profession, and one I will never forget.

I couldn't help thinking that if most people could witness this scene, they might think twice about donating their bodies. Just the thought of my organs being scattered on silver trays around a science laboratory gave me the chills! Interns would be getting in their training hours on my body parts, and in the long run, somebody was going to make money on me!

On the other hand, if my body parts were worth something to the family I left behind, then perhaps, even in death, reduced to segments on a silver tray, I could still accomplish something worthwhile.

A CADAVER BROKER

In Carlsbad, California, there is a unique laboratory

that helps doctors practice their surgical techniques on such cadaver specimens as severed shoulders and knees. What's unusual is that a sports-oriented brace manufacturer operates the lab. Smith & Nephew Donjoy allows doctors in private practice to gain access to this lab, something rarely possible with medical school laboratories.

According to a company spokesperson, surgeons using the lab pay only a nominal fee, which covers little more than the costs of cadavers. Exactly how the company obtains the cadaver parts was something the spokesperson declined to discuss, except to say that it purchases carefully screened tissue "from one of the largest medical schools in Southern California."[2]

ON SALE AT YOUR HMO: ORGAN TRANSPLANTS

Not just ordinary people are looking for organs; now your local health maintenance organization (HMO) is shopping around for the best price.

"Discount fever is hitting the high end of medicine: the organ-transplant business," the *Wall Street Journal* reported in a 17 January 1995 article. Leading centers of transplants such as Cleveland Clinic, Duke, and Johns Hopkins Universities are reducing prices by up to 60 percent, hoping to win big contracts with HMOs and other large insurers. These contracts include the cost of obtaining donor organs (which themselves cannot be sold), surgery, drugs, and follow-up care.

The rate for a heart transplant, previously listed at $200,000, has dropped as low as $110,000, while bone marrow transplants have fallen to $65,000, compared to the previous 1994 average of $172,000. Aiding the price cutting is new medical technology that permits discharging patients sooner and having them finish their care in less expensive outpatient locations.

Here is a summary of U.S. transplant costs for five organs.[3]

THE COST OF TRANSPLANTS

Organ	No. of Transplants Per Year *	List Prices **	Discounted Prices
Kidneys	10,928	$92,700	$50,000 to 60,000
Bone Marrow	6,300	172,900	65,000
Livers	3,442	280,200	150,000 to 200,000
Hearts	2,298	222,700	110,000
Lungs	664	265,100	130,000

* Number of transplants is for 1993.
** Prices are for 1995.

PENIS PARTS FOR SALE
(NO LORENA BOBBITS—PLEASE!)

There are a few places in America that are doing research with skin, both natural and synthetic. There's one in California that is currently buying or bartering from hospitals and universities a rather unusual commodity—clippings from circumcised babies. Since the skin has to be living, it must be preserved quickly and put on ice. It is then transferred to Advanced Tissue Sciences in La Jolla, which specializes in products made of living human skin. The firm is now using the children's foreskin to make tissue that will help severe burn victims, people with skin ulcers, and other wound victims. The company is working with other body parts and organs, including cartilage and an artificially grown liver.

Advanced Tissue Sciences is just one of many biotech companies that are trying to transplant specific cells and tissues that they have engineered in the laboratory. Some researchers are even talking of growing organs in petri dishes, says *Business Week*. Though this work faces tough regulatory issues, Advanced Tissue Sciences expects this work will continue "because these treatments address horrible conditions such as organ failure, or severe burns that are now inadequately treated."[4]

Skin is also used in other kinds of medical research. Because of its important barrier function, skin is often needed to test drugs and cosmetics that are applied to skin. Previously, many such tests for toxicity and irritancy were done on animals.

GIVING THE GIFT OF LIFE

Sometimes we must consider giving. In this day and age, there are more than 39,000 people registered as waiting for organ transplants, according to the National Organ Procurement and Transplantation Network. It is estimated that 3,000 of these people die each year because no suitable organs can be found.

Much remains to be done if these statistics are to improve. A recent study by the Harvard School of Public Health and the Partnership for Organ Donation examined more than 40,000 medical records from 100 hospitals, hunting potential organ donations that were missed.

The researchers found that hospitals often do a poor job of identifying potential donors and fail to inform local organ banks of potential donors, and they also found that doctors often do a poor job of requesting donations. In 20 percent of the cases studied, doctors raised the idea of organ donations at the same time they first informed the family that the patient was brain dead. In these cases, 75 percent of those asked said no.

In Pittsburgh, the Center for Organ Recovery and Education hired three phone operators and told hospitals to call whenever death was imminent for any patient. Phone calls grew from 300 to 15,000 in two years, and donations rose by 75 percent. Another group at the University of Kentucky found that it took too long to declare brain death. The process was reduced to hours from days, and organ-bank coordinators rather than doctors were called in to explain the process to families. As a result, the number of donors almost doubled.

Also helping to ease the national crisis have been the use of donor sticker cards on motor vehicle licenses, and the use of 800 numbers to increase public awareness. Similar campaigns are under way in Canada to help ease organ shortages there.

In one other study, it was found that many medical examiners were refusing to release organs from the dead, fearing that they might lose needed evidence in legal cases. The report, carried in the *Journal of the American Medical Association*, stated that many lives were lost because these organs were withheld. Yet the researchers found that in areas of the country where medical examiners routinely release organs, no legal case has ever suffered.

RESOURCE LIST

The following is a resource list of where you can donate your body or body parts. All donations are accepted.

American Red Cross National Tissue Service
4050 Lindell Boulevard
St. Louis, MO 63108
1-800-2-TISSUE or (314) 289-1155
The Red Cross is widely known for its humanitarian efforts. It is on the scene after floods, earthquakes, and other disasters, and in addition to its blood banks, it maintains more than 40 Red Cross Tissue Centers nationwide. Serving thousands every year, this organization makes it possible for recipients to see, hear,

Body for Sale

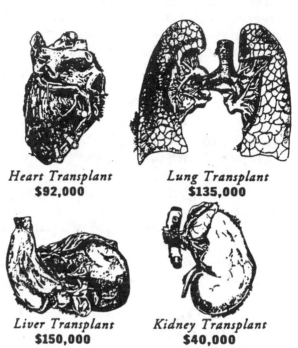

Heart Transplant
$92,000

Lung Transplant
$135,000

Liver Transplant
$150,000

Kidney Transplant
$40,000

WHAT YOU NEED TO SEE THIS AD
CAN'T BE REPLACED WITH ANY AMOUNT OF MONEY

The National Society to Prevent Blindness has been funding eye research for more than 60 years. While our scientists have been successful in curing various eye disorders, replacing the human eye is still impossible.

That's why we have more than 30 different programs to help preserve sight. In fact, last year alone we prevented sight loss in more than 90,000 people.

Call 1-800-331-2020 to help us keep you doing what you're doing now. Seeing.

❈ NATIONAL SOCIETY TO PREVENT BLINDNESS®
With Your Help, We Make Miracles.

84

walk—and live. You can contact it for further information. Body donations are accepted.

The National Kidney Foundation, Inc.
30 East 33rd St.
New York, NY 10016
1-800-747-5527 or (212) 889-2210
This nonprofit foundation helps millions who suffer from kidney disease by providing education, information, research, and patient services. If you are interested in becoming a donor, contact it for more detailed information.

Eye Bank Association of America
1725 Eye St, N.W., Suite 308
Washington, D.C. 20006-2403
(202) 775-4999
The Eye Bank is a nonprofit corporation dedicated to research, education, and the preservation of sight through the collection, processing, and distribution of human ocular tissue. It maintains a center for the diagnostic evaluation and therapy of ocular disease for the physician community and general public.

LifeBanc
909 E. 101st St.
Cleveland, OH 44106
1-800-558-LIFE or (216) 791-5433
LifeBanc is a nonprofit donor organization. It runs a toll-free hot line for anyone with questions about organ tissue donations. This group provides free key rings that sport the slogan "Key to Life."

The Living Bank
P.O. Box 6725
Houston, TX 77625
1-800-528-2971 or (713) 528-2971

A nonprofit organization, TLB maintains the largest computerized multiorgan and tissue donor registry in the world, serving all 50 states and six foreign countries.

National Marrow Donor Program
3433 Broadway St., N.E.
Minneapolis, MN 55413
(612) 378-2044
A nonprofit organization, NMDP has an international computerized data bank to match potential donors with patients in need of bone marrow transplants. If you are interested in becoming a donor, you can request a list of the nearest centers.

National Temporal Bone Banks Program
Eye and Ear Infirmary
243 Charles St.
Boston, MA 02114
(617) 573-3711
This program is administered by the nonprofit Deafness Research Foundation. If you are hearing impaired and are interested in donating temporal bone for use in research, contact the NTBBP.

United Network for Organ Sharing (UNOS)
1100 Boulders Parkway, Suite 500
P.O. Box 13770
Richmond, Virginia 23225-8770
1-800-24-DONOR
UNOS has one of the largest listings for people on waiting lists for organ transplants. It has computers interlinked throughout the world and is always in need of organs and tissue.

NOTES

1. Rex Dalton, "Half-skeletons target of probe here," *San Diego Union-Tribune*, (3 February 1995): A-1.

2. Bruce Bigelow, "Inside the joint," *San Diego Union-Tribune* (16 December 1994): E-1.

3. G. Anders, "On sale now at your HMO: Organ transplants," *Wall Street Journal* (17 January 1995): B-1.

4. "Miracle Cures May Be in Your Cells," *Business Week* (6 December 1993): 76.

About the Author

Ed Brassard is uniquely qualified to reveal eye-opening truths about the controversial medical industry. As a coordinator for a high-tech research firm and a human subject for research in numerous medical research studies, his behind-the-scene experiences in laboratories, hospitals, and pharmaceutical companies give him an uncommonly broad perspective on this front-page issue.

Brassard has recently been profiled on the front page of the *San Diego Union-Tribune* for his role in medical research studies and has been interviewed on various eye-opening subjects by the *Los Angeles Times*, the *National Enquirer*, and the producers of CBS' *Eye to Eye*. Brassard is also listed in the *Guinness Book of World Records* and *Ripley's Believe It or Not*.